CONFESSIONS
OF A SLOW TWO-MILER

**A Horse Racing Memoir by
MATT SHEPPARD**

All rights reserved. No part of this publication may be reproduced, stored in a retrieval system, transmitted, or utilised in any form or by any means electronic, mechanical, photocopying, recording audio or visual, or otherwise, without written prior permission of the copyright owner.

Copyright © Matt Sheppard, 2024
First published in Great Britain in 2024

ISBN 978-1-915899-06-4

The right of Matt Sheppard to be identified as the Author of this work has been asserted by him in accordance with the Copyright, Designs and Patents Acts 1988.

A CIP catalogue record for this book is available from the British Library.

Published by Weatherbys Ltd in conjunction with Matt Sheppard, this book is produced entirely in the UK and is available to order from Weatherbys Shop, www.weatherbysshop.co.uk and other outlets:

Weatherbys Ltd
Sanders Road
Wellingborough
Northamptonshire
NN8 4BX
United Kingdom
www.weatherbys.co.uk

All attempts have been made to contact photograph copyright holders wherever possible

Disclaimer

Every effort has been made to ensure the accuracy of the information contained in this publication. All content provided is the responsibility of the author. The author has been advised to ensure that every effort has been made to trace or contact all copyright holders. The author has stated to the publishers that the contents of this book are true. Neither the publisher nor the author can accept responsibility for any errors or omissions, particularly where horses change ownership or trainers after the publication has gone to print. The author and publishers disclaim, as far as the law allows, any liability arising directly or indirectly from the use, or misuse, of any information contained in this book.

Any veterinary information in this book is based on the author's personal observation, research or experience and should not be relied upon as a substitute for professional advice. In some limited cases, the names of people or details of places or events have been changed to protect the privacy of others.

The thoughts, opinions and content of this book are that of the author and do not reflect the views and opinions of Weatherbys Ltd.

DESIGNED, PRODUCED AND PUBLISHED BY WEATHERBYS

This book is dedicated to my wife Nicky, who receives few mentions but has been by my side all the way.

CONTENTS

	Foreword	7
	Preface	9
1	Early Days (and Thank God I Escaped Farming!)	13
2	The Quality of Mercy and Life-Saving in Corfu	19
3	Flat Racing at Whatcombe and a Lucky Escape!	25
4	Mind Reading in Kildare (and Moore Experience)	28
5	The Only Way is Eastnor	41
6	The Golden Age of Point-to-Points	44
7	Matt Sheppard: Racehorse Trainer	48
8	Gone With The Wind & Other Equine Issues	56
9	Staying on the Carousel: Surviving the Business of Training	61
10	Training Owners	68
11	Horses for Courses: A 'Who's Who' of Eastnor's Hall of Fame	77
12	Jockeys, Then and Now	95
13	Staff	102
14	The Owner from Hell	105
15	The Owner from Heaven	115
16	Some Thoughts on Gamblers and Greed	127
17	My Race Riding Career (A Short Chapter!)	130
18	Media	132
19	How to Become a Racehorse Trainer in the 2020s	135
20	Covid-19 2020-22 Lockdown (and Post-Lockdown) Diary	145
21	Killer Chairs and 'The Slow Two-Miler'	165
	Appendix 1 – Eastnor winners	173
	Acknowledgements	184

FOREWORD

By Racing Journalist and Author Neil Clark

In the early 2000s I became 'John Bull', the Midland correspondent of the *Racing and Football Outlook* newspaper. My job entailed writing a weekly column on the best bets from Midlands racing stables. I was given a list of trainers situated in my patch. And that's how I became friends with Matt Sheppard. I would ring Matt up almost every Sunday morning to find out the latest news from his yard. He was always friendly and helpful and 'Home Farm' provided me with a rich source of decent-priced winners, which helped me win the naps table twice and come within a short head of doing so on other occasions.

I soon began to realise that Matt was a greatly underrated trainer. Invariably he would manage to improve horses that came to him from other stables, or 'Eastnor' them to use his own term to describe the process.

I remember tipping San Marco when he won at 16/1 on his first outing for Matt at Worcester on Derby Day 2004. Then there was little Rabbit, who ran up a sequence in the summer of 2006, rising 24 pounds in the handicap. I had napped Rabbit in a race at Stratford but didn't know the result for a few days as, believe it or not, I was travelling on the Trans-Siberian railway. Lo and behold, when I finally managed to log into a computer (it was the days before smartphones) I found out she had won at 6/1.

Another 'Sheppard special' was Allez Toujours. I remember ringing Matt up in the week before the Simon Gegg-owned chaser was due to run at Uttoxeter. Matt told me his gelding was 'as fit as f...' so I made it my nap of the week. Result, Allez Toujours was never headed and won at 10/1. Rated only 58, it was the lowest-rated horse Matt ever trained to win a race, but it was a very sweet victory for me. In twenty years of following Matt's yard there have been some wonderful moments and inevitably, given the nature of the game, some sad ones too. The worst was undoubtedly when dear old Asparagus, a big stable favourite, collapsed and died after running an absolute blinder in the Welsh Grand National of 2004.

By contrast one of the best memories happened a few weeks before that when Smile Pleeze stayed on strongly up the Cheltenham hill to land the amateur riders' handicap at the November meeting. Despite finishing a staying-on fourth over a 2f shorter trip at the same course a few weeks earlier at odds of 25/1 Smile Pleeze was allowed to go off at 16/1 on the day. It was my father's birthday and I took him to Cheltenham as his present. Not only did we both back the winner, I also told our next door neighbour to back him too just before leaving. Everyone was smiling that night!

In the current tough climate it's harder than ever to make it pay as a jumps trainer, especially when prize money has been so low and nearly all the top horses are concentrated in a very small number of training establishments. But Matt has managed to survive and is still in there punching above his weight and producing winners. His life story is full of ups and downs but his good humour shines through it all. He modestly calls himself 'A Slow Two Miler', but if so, he's one slow two miler I'd quite happily have a bet on, whatever the going. Enjoy this fascinating account of life at the coalface of National Hunt racing.

*Neil Clark's latest book *Champion Jump Horse Racing Jockeys from 1945 to the Present Day* is published by White Owl Books.

PREFACE

When I started this project, it had been on my mind for many years. The Covid lockdown gave me the nudge to get started. I wrote the second last paragraph first and memories flowed from there. In the 2021/22 season events proved once again the highs and lows of our sport and lifestyle, with Not Available proving to be a shrewd purchase and our son Stan hitting the big time with Welsh Grand National success for Sam Thomas and a Betfair Hurdle winner for his boss Tom Lacey. Stan's position as stable jockey has been hard earned and we are very proud of him. My new title is "Stan Sheppard's dad".

Many of my thoughts and theories have no scientific or veterinary evidence but sometimes my horsemanship and experience screams to me those certain things when you are dealing with a racehorse in training which just don't add up.

Regardless of all my musings I am still training and intend to be for a good while yet. In that 2021/22 National Hunt season I posted eleven winners from 86 runners and £106,000 prize money put me in the top hundred UK trainers, which I consider to be a big deal. Putin and all the world's woes will not stop me, I hope.

***

March 2020. The Covid-19 Nightmare was about to kick off. In February I had met with my financial advisor, and both Nicky's and my pensions were flourishing. I had done some calculations around what we both were probably going to inherit, and I worked out that with a little luck, I should be able to retire from being a racehorse trainer at 60, and semi-retire from working altogether. My owners were getting old and passing on, and all those years of working 80+ hours a week were beginning to tell. When you get to a stage in life when you think that only working five hours in a day instead of ten hours a day is a day off, you know something is wrong somewhere. When Mrs Shep (mainly Mrs Shep) and I are riding the cranky nags because the staff are not good enough or unwilling to sit on a young wild beast and they all drive better cars than I have ever owned, thoughts of 'WTF am I doing?' surface near the top of my thoughts daily. My body was failing: I had one new artificial hip and the other one was giving up. It's a young man's game! I was thinking that the next pair of shoes I buy needed to be slip-ons!

When I turned 50 I thought that I would be lucky to still be in business at 55, but I had an influx of horses and new owners and it proved to be boom time. Well, boom for business turnover and loads of staff, but despite The Bay Birch raising our profile no other racehorses of any note. Hitting 55 and losing owner Simon Gegg who passed away coupled with the Covid crisis told me that unless I attract a new proper racing enthusiast to support Matt Sheppard Racing then things were going to be tough.

No matter what happens next in my life, I cannot complain. It has been a great ride and I am very lucky to have enjoyed it.

Anyway, here I was, at 55 years old. The Bay Birch, the best horse I've ever trained, had won a chase off a handicap mark of 145 and at 152 was the highest rated horse ever to be trained at Eastnor. She had just run at the Cheltenham Festival in the Grand Annual and had finished a respectable eighth out of eighteen, only beaten twelve lengths. I had set my son Stan up with a career as a professional jump jockey and with some luck and hard work he should make a decent living.

I had set myself four goals to achieve before I turned 60:
1. Semi-retire from work, and retire from training.
2. Train 200 National Hunt winners
3. Reach £2 million in prize money
4. Escape with no debt

Covid turned most of those goals upside down.

200 winners by 2025 could probably be achieved, but my pension took a knock and current prize money levels will make it a struggle to reach my £2million goal.

This account of my life is going to explain exactly how it all started. It will detail what I have endured and how I have reached where I am. I hope it will not put anyone off being involved in the awesome sport of Horse Racing! It has been work hard, play hard all the way, and I am very proud of what I have achieved.

There is no diversity in this book. That is just the way my life has been lived. There is not much political correctness either. But that is just me! There is no sex in the book either, as it would be fiction, but some of the tales described here you could not have made up anyway.

Throughout, tongue straps will have multiple mentions. Whoever was the first trainer to identify that strapping a racehorse's tongue to the bottom jaw doesn't appear to get a mention in racing folklore. Most horses tolerate the unnatural addition with little resistance. That a short length of lady's nylon stocking can improve racecourse performance on certain horses has proven to be a game changer.

Anybody reading this account may come to the conclusion that I am bonkers. All the heartache and grief, disappointments and falls are far outweighed by the highs and joyful times. A motto of my life is 'if you can't do a job that makes money, do a job that saves money (or keeps you warm)'. Whether it is cutting your own birch for the schooling fences or, as my compulsion is, to collect firewood, all year round. Little things that keep the meagre finances within a sensible debt free boundary. They would probably be right, a certain amount of craziness is needed, but I'm not sure a real job would suit me after all this time.

CHAPTER 1

EARLY DAYS (AND THANK GOD I ESCAPED FARMING!)

I was born in Wells, Somerset in March 1965, where we lived until I was seven. Then my family upped sticks in search of a bigger farm to Llangorse in Breconshire in Wales. Our East Horrington dairy farm of 130 acres was OK to milk 40 cows, but to milk 60 cows cheaper land in Wales meant that 220 acres could be purchased.

I was the eldest of four children (three English born and one Welsh born). My father was a dairy farmer. Now that IS hard work – and all of the Work Hard with none of the Play Hard! Luckily for me and my siblings, he could see there was no future for us in farming at that scale. In fact he did everything he could to put me off! He sold his herd and set up a very successful holiday cottage business. I did go to the Welsh Agricultural College in Aberystwyth, but after six months of my gap year spent in New Zealand, I never returned.

We always had horses and ponies as kids. Pony Club and hunting was my background. My parents always had loads of ponies and it was in a golden era when every village had an agricultural show with a horse and pony section. We would arrive in time for the first classes of the day in our old Bedford TK wooden horsebox with about nine ponies squeezed in the back. They would be unloaded, bridled up and tied to a rope around the lorry and we would switch the saddles between mounts as they were required for specific classes. Very often father would get to the beer tent and as we gave him envelopes with our winning prize money he would supply more cash to enter and have another cider. Toni, my sister, and I thought we were amazing. We just turned up at the weekend, jumped on these semi-feral ponies and would sweep the board. Much later in life it dawned on me that our parents employed Terry, an older strong teenager who spent the week days nagging and schooling up the ponies whilst we were at school, ready to perform at the shows.

I rode in my first point-to-point ride on my sixteenth birthday. I fell off. Mainly my riding ability was very moderate. It was in March 1981 at the Brecon Point-to-Point, a rearranged midweek fixture. I went to school in the morning and then rode Hecho in the maiden race.

Mr. and Mrs. P. J. Sheppard and son Mathew watch a race in progress.

Pony Club

Chapter 1

Hecho was a maiden all his life. That means he never won a race. But he was a regular on the Welsh racing circuit for many years. He would turn up every week or fortnight with all sorts of different riders and usually completed safely in third or fourth spot. I wasn't really ready and old Hecho sussed straight away that I was just a passenger and duly dumped me into the open ditch.

I rode at the Welsh fixtures for the next five seasons and was fairly intimidated by some of the other jockeys. They didn't seem to be very gentlemanly amateur riders to me. I was a mild-mannered laid-back student with long blond hair and my fellow riders included steel workers from Port Talbot, welders and coal miners. In all, some very hard men, fabulous riders in an age when not every young rider was a wannabe professional jockey – with the exception of Carl Llewellyn, who went on to win the Grand National in 1992 on Party Politics. In the jockeys' changing room every saddle was a docker, that is a light-weight small saddle to enable a heavy jockey to make the minimum weight of twelve stone.

A point-to-point jockeys' changing room is now full of big heavy saddles and fit young stable lads and lasses. On one occasion at the Brecon Hunt Point-to-Point at Llanfrynach, top rider Dai Jones, who could do the weight comfortably, sat on the scales for his own ride and then requested to triple weigh for his next two mounts as well. That was number 5 in the restricted race and number 10 in the first maiden. Without looking up the amateur clerk of the scales ticked the necessary boxes and the runners were weighed out. However the other two mounts were for John Tudor and Tim Jones who were always struggling with their ability to make the weight. It would be a serious breach of the rules today, but back then it was true amateur cavalier behaviour. I caught up with Tim recently to confirm the tale. He said that it was true, but very often they had to select a different stand-in jockey to weigh because Dai Jones was a fat bastard too. He also presented his sister Pip to weigh out for him on more than one occasion, which is even more of a cheek. There was a hunt in South Wales called the Banwen Miners who held a meeting at Erw Lon in Carmarthenshire and I can guarantee there were no toffs or gentry hunting with that pack of hounds.

I spent my late teenage years in the Sixth Form and did a work experience year at a local farm that happened to have a couple of point-to-pointers before going off to Aberystwyth to the Welsh Agricultural College for the first term of a diploma course. I had a chance to spend six months of my gap year working in New Zealand and duly set off with my pal Glyn: two young lads from the Brecon Beacons off to see the world.

We set off from Heathrow, rucksacks crammed with kit. There was no social media or any easy quick way contacting home back then and when we arrived at our placements it was Stone Age to say the least. On the way we landed in Bombay and again at Sydney before arriving in Auckland 28 hours after we started. We caught a bus to the centre of town in search of the Youth Hostel and we clearly looked out of place because numerous passers-by asked if they could help. We checked in, found the nearest Chinese restaurant and ordered a feast but failed to eat a mouthful. Our jet lag caught up with us and made our appetites disappear.

Rural Kiwi was almost third world compared to the UK. The farms were remote in location even before they were spread out. A social life was hard to achieve and it seemed as if the highlight of the month was the dog dosing event which took place at a crossroads in the middle of nowhere. The authorities needed to have a strategy to eliminate a disease called Hydatids from the population. It was caused by sheepdogs eating contaminated sheep meat, worm eggs passing through the animal and attaching themselves on to the dog's tails and then being transferred by brushing on to the hands of humans and entering the humans (mainly children) in the form of troublesome cysts all over the human body.

The creation of dog dosing was an effective way to reduce the spread of this serious disease. All the sheep farmers within an extensive area would collect at a location to meet a vet who would feed a pill to all the local dogs to eradicate the worm. On the said day farmers would arrive in their pickups with their entire families and a whole pack of dogs to meet the vet. A crate of beer was a compulsory inclusion and no one went home until all the beer was drunk. The wives gossiped with all the other wives, the farmers complained about farming and all the children, young and old, played and met. The hot bitches all got covered and expanded the gene pool. It was the biggest day of the month.

The Kiwi farmers showed us a great time and we were welcome everywhere. After working four and a half months we had purchased an old Hillman Hunter (calling a car a Hunter would lead to cancellation in these absurd, politically correct times) car and set off for six weeks touring the country before we returned. There was a network of farmers who would put us for up for a couple of days in return for a day's work and show us the

In Kiwi

Snake Charming in Singapore

local sites and lock up their daughters. All the farmers were still smarting from the fact that the UK had dumped on our Commonwealth partners by signing up to the European Economic Community. New Zealand supplied the UK with food during and after the Second World War and endured rationing afterwards and were miffed by such a betrayal. It was 1986, only 41 years after VE day.

We returned from Kiwi in January via Singapore and I was due to complete my gap year working for the Johnson family (as in champion jockey Richard Johnson's family) at Madley. The job would have entailed arable farm work along with helping out with the family racehorses, but whilst I was away Keith Johnson suffered a serious farming accident and although he recovered the family put their training interests on hold, so the job no longer existed. I then found a job milking cows near Hay-on-Wye and continued to ride in point-to-points including my first winner on a horse called Light Snacks in the Brecon Hunt race in 1986. I was 21 years old and I was soon to be given a chance to consider a change of career.

CHAPTER 2

THE QUALITY OF MERCY AND LIFE-SAVING IN CORFU

When a jockey friend of mine lost his driving licence and needed wheels, he found me a job at Mrs Mercy Rimell's at Kinnersley Stables in Upton-on-Severn.

I absolutely loved it. I met Nicky, my future wife, out hunting with the Ledbury, and I rode some local winners point-to-pointing. I lived my life to the full, burning the candle at both ends. I have always been good in the mornings. Mrs Rimell was a formidable woman. One of her favourite phrases was: 'If they don't like it, they know what they can do! They can Fuck Off!"

I still use that one today myself...

Mercy got me into trouble on one occasion. On a Friday in the middle of winter, a horse I looked after called Celtic Flight had an engagement in a late afternoon novice chase at Kempton. I rode the horse daily and felt that the horse was in good form and was expecting him to run a good race. Mercy didn't travel to Kempton herself, which was very unusual, so the assistant trainer drove down to saddle it and Dermot Browne was jocked-up to ride. I fully accept that I was young and knew very little but the jockey gave it no ride whatsoever. There was no satellite racing television channels back then so Mercy only had the report from the assistant. On Saturday Madam found me out and declared, 'I hear your horse didn't run very well yesterday, Matthew?' To which I replied, 'It didn't get much of a ride, Madam'.

The next I hear is Mercy searching out Dermot who was tacking up and barking 'Dermot, Dermot, Matthew said that you didn't give that horse much of a ride.' Which made things tricky for a while. Dermot's reputation subsequently went downhill when he got into bad company and ended up being warned off for being the 'Needleman' responsible for administering sedatives to favourites for gambling purposes. He disappeared from the scene, but in a bizarre incident I met him again circa 1990. Nicky and I were working in Kildare and housesitting for an acquaintance and went out for supper at a remote restaurant that we had never visited before somewhere near Moone. All the tables were vacant except for one which had two diners, Dermot Browne and not the head honcho but someone very near the top of the Turf Club. Digital phone cameras were 30 years away but unless you saw it you wouldn't have believed it. Dermot was, and still is, well warned off.

It was the last three years of Mrs Rimell's career, but Gaye Brief, the 1983 Champion Hurdle Winner, was still around, Gala's Image won an Arkle with Richard Linley dislocating his shoulder after the last, and Celtic Chief was right up there too, finishing second in two Champion Hurdles. I was lucky enough to ride four wins on a horse called Deep Prospect. He had been top lot at the Tattersalls Derby sale at Fairyhouse, but after he had disappointed under Rules Sheikh Ali Abu Khamsin, the owner, had him back to his stud in Devon. At Christmas, Mrs Rimell had gone to visit for lunch, and asked about the horse. The Sheikh said, 'I will give him to you as a Christmas gift!'

The next day Clifford Rawlings, the travelling head lad, was sent down to collect him, and Mrs Rimell was announcing to everyone how she had got me a point-to-pointer to ride.

We had to organise him to go hunting seven times in order to qualify quickly and get to the track for the first local Garnons meeting, where he had to run in the restricted race. Talk about bolt up! He pulled so hard my arms ached for the next two days! Another easy win followed at Chaddesley Corbett, followed by a hunter chase at Worcester where he won again. By then the ground was drying up, and he was turned out at grass.

When it started raining again, he was retrieved from the field to run in the John Corbett Cup, the novice hunter chase final at Stratford at the end of the season, which we won.

Within a couple of weeks, Deep Prospect was sold and away. Mrs Rimell gave me £200 cash, with which I bought a new suit and went on holiday with Nicky – which incidentally prompts its own story...

It was my first ever foreign beach holiday. I think the whole package for a week in Corfu came to £90 each. The highlight, perhaps not what you'd expect from a sun, sea and sand break, was saving a drowning man from the sea. Fed up with lying in the sun doing nothing, I was sitting up scanning the immediate area looking for sights. The beach was a gentle slope into a very still bay with any real depth of water a long way out. A bather came into view. He was face down in about four feet of water and as far as I could tell, maybe had goggles on and was looking at whatever maybe on the seabed. I was puzzled because I had already learnt that there was nothing to see. No fish or crabs or anything. All the sea life was to be seen in the rocky area in front of the cliffs at the peripherals of the bay.

Divine Charger, £50 Best Turned Out Award 1986!

Me riding Sally Potheen to win at Talybont point-to-point

Celebrating Three Counties' Cheltenham Foxhunters win, Kinnersley 1989. I'm in the cowboy hat.

After winning 1988 John Corbet at Stratford – *courtesy of Jim Meads*

Anyway, he got closer and I thought maybe he had a snorkel but closer he got and still nothing was obvious. Concerned, I waded out to check for sure, got closer and tapped the man on the shoulder. No response! I reached under his chin and pulled him over on to his back to see a lifeless, blue face. Hollering like a mad thing I dragged him to the shore and half way up the beach (it's amazing how strong you are when push comes to shove). My CPR skills were non-existent back then but a fit topless mature German woman (what today would be referred to as a MILF) left her sunbed, straddled our casualty and successfully revived him. She wanted to award me a 'medallion'. Some policemen turned up with a trestle table as a stretcher and carted him away. I didn't hear any more about the incident but there was no inquiry or police type-questions.

I digress.

My future wife Nicky Guilding first came to my attention in possibly 1981 at Croome and West Warwick Point-to-Point at Upton-upon-Severn on Easter Tuesday. In the golden years of pointing this particular fixture was a must for the hunt racing community. The meeting would always have a huge crowd with for some top class sport. The meeting has since lost its unique date and prestige due to many factors. Easter Tuesday is no longer considered part of the Bank Holiday weekend and the West Midlands working class holiday crowd no longer have it in their diaries. Also it is a struggle to get helpers on the day, as so many of the usual hunt followers have to work on that day and there are even fewer to help tidy up on the Wednesday.

Anyhow, the Sheppard family went to the fixture and I noted Nicky riding a horse called Pacify for her family in the Ladies race. The commentator Jeremy Branfoot was a Guilding family friend and made much of the fact that she was the daughter of local pointing legend Roger Guilding. I'm not sure of the result of the race, but I did some homework in the McKenzie and Selby point-to-point form books and learned some of her heritage.

I didn't actually meet her in person until 1986, when I started work for Mercy Rimell. I was out hunting with the Ledbury qualifying a pointer. Mercy's granddaughter, Katie, was with me and suggested I catch up with the girl on 'the big horse', and see if I could blag an invite to her 21st birthday party, which was that night. I trotted up behind and looked up from my much smaller mount and said, 'My name is Matt and please may I come to your party?' to which she answered 'Yes'. I remember the night for one particular event, perhaps not the one you would expect. Another girl (who later proved to be a successful trainer) wrote her telephone number (only landlines back then) on my chest in lipstick. I never did dial it!

***

Schooling a reluctant juvenile hurdler, the closer to the obstacle the slower the horse moved, the harder I pushed and slapped and shunted. The spectacle was not at all stylish or particularly effective. On a successful but ungainly clearance of the line of hurdles, I returned to where Mercy was watching and was greeted by 'Matthew, you were riding like a dog fucking a box of nails.'

Deep Prospect winning at Stratford, led in by Colin Parker.

CHAPTER 3

FLAT RACING AT WHATCOMBE AND A LUCKY ESCAPE!

During the summer of 1987 I worked for Paul Cole at Whatcombe, between Wantage and Hungerford. Michael Bell, the Derby winning trainer, was assistant trainer and I had looked after his hunter chaser Ten Cherries at Mrs Rimell's. He got me the job, which proved to be an interesting summer. At nine stone seven pounds in weight I was considered too heavy to ride work on the flat horses, but fit young riders like me were considered cannon fodder to sit on fractious two-year-olds to ride to the gallops and back with the work riders doing the important level weights assessments.

I have three main memories as follows:

At very short notice I was asked to go overnight to lead up at Pontefract. The horse was called Broken Hearted, who proved to be a classy type and a relatively successful sire. Willie Carson rode the horse to win on his debut by so far that that he had unsaddled and weighed in before the runners-up even got to the winners enclosure! The horse went on to win the Extel Handicap at Goodwood in his three-year-old season and at four had some mighty battles with Mtoto.

At Whatcombe that summer I also met an Irish lad called Barty. He had worked in plenty of Irish yards and thought he would get some UK experience. He was very keen to become my new best friend, mainly because I had wheels and Barty loved to have a bet. These were the days when on-course betting or betting shops were the only options.

One particular Saturday, Barty was very anxious to make the betting shop in plenty of time so we duly teamed up and parked in a carpark adjacent to the one in Wantage. Barty produced a selection of semi filled-in betting slips. He had his transistor radio tuned into RTE (Radio Television Eireann) and knew that the day's Irish non-runners were reported at a regular slot every Saturday during the sports update. Barty listened to the list and noted the late race non-runners. He filled in two later non-runners on the bottom of the betting slip. He then listened to the first broadcast race, filled in the winning horse and hot-footed it in to place his bet. Because of lack of interest in the Irish racing, the non-runner information was very slow to filter through, as were the results. There were no live pictures, only UK commentary. Barty placed his bet as a treble, with his first selection having already won and the

Venetia Williams (far left), Johnny Greenall (far right) and me leading on Bent Deal. Very rare photo of me looking stylish over a fence.

later selections non-runners. Because it included later races, the teller taking the bet would have not been too concerned with the timings. BOOM! A certain winner, and I think Barty had three winning Saturdays before on his next visit to the betting shop he was greeted by a police officer and told in no uncertain terms to bugger off and never return. It was a clever idea and fair play to Barty for dreaming it up, but when I meet Barty at the sales or racing, he is still searching for the next get rich quick scheme to feather his nest.

On 19 August 1987 I changed my daily routine. I was living in small flat on site at Whatcombe and every day at lunchtime I went down the drive and turned left for Wantage. On this day for no particular reason I turned right for Hungerford. Maybe because someone had recommended the motor factors shop, but I don't recall! So I drove into Hungerford, parked at the top end of the High Street and purchased some windscreen wipers for my Talbot Horizon. I fitted them on to the car, treated myself to some lunchtime fish and chips and sat on a bench to eat them wearing a bright orange t-shirt. Fish and chips devoured, I hopped back in the car and headed out of town.

As I made my way out of town, multiple police cars were screaming in the opposite direction. I got back to Whatcombe, grabbed forty winks and awoke to learn that Michael Ryan had made Hungerford famous for one of the darkest days in recent UK history, gunning down sixteen people! I was so near yet so far, and in my orange t-shirt I would have been a juicy target!

At the end of my third season at Kinnersley Mrs Rimell retired, and through some friends of Nicky's parents I managed to get a job as assistant trainer to Arthur Moore in the Republic of Ireland.

CHAPTER 4

MIND READING IN KILDARE
(AND MOORE EXPERIENCE)

I started working for Arthur Moore in Kildare in the autumn of 1989. He had a huge reputation as a jumps trainer-come-horse dealer in Ireland. He was certainly bred for the part. His father Dan, from whom he learnt his trade, had been a multiple Cheltenham Festival winning trainer, associated with many top-class horses. The most famous was the great L'Escargot, who not only won back-to-back Gold Cups in the early 1970s but then, as a twelve-year-old, beat Red Rum (not many horses did that!) in the 1975 Grand National. Dan also trained Tied Cottage, probably the most unlucky horse never to win a Cheltenham Gold Cup. While his father was still training Arthur had won the Irish Grand National as an amateur rider on King's Sprite in 1971. As a trainer in the late 1980s he was setting up a powerful string just as the Irish economy was beginning to prosper enough so that the good horses could be retained by Irish connections rather than needing to be sold to the UK.

1989-1992

After three years at Kinnersley working in a fairly traditional old-fashioned yard, the Republic of Ireland was eye-opening. After being a stable lad-cum pupil assistant-trainer in the UK, the Irish system was very different. Kinnersley would start at 7am, muck out three or four, ride out the first lot, breakfast 9am, sweep up, ride out two more lots (rarely three), then groom the horses. At evening stables Mrs Rimell, if not away racing, would inspect the groomed horses, stripped, make a mental note of the horses' condition and weight and decide on its training regime for the future days. Also, the staff consisted of lots of old-timers who had been in the industry for many years.

By contrast, when I started at Dereens, we had up to 70 horses, with fewer than twenty stable staff, all teenagers except for myself and two others: Pat Malone and Jim Sheridan. We started at 8am and worked through until we were finished! There was plenty of roadwork, but rural Irish roads were not busy and very safe. Early exercise included, 'Let's now trot up this hill'. Bearing in mind I had been bought up in mid-Wales just under the Black Mountains, I did look puzzled when the hill in question was in fact up and over a railway bridge.

Chapter 4

A favourite trick among the lads was to listen out for trains and ensure that the visiting random Saturday morning work-rider was spot-on in the middle of the bridge when the train went under. They would even pull sky-hooks to try and get the train driver to sound his horn. The Saturday riders were generally on a safe horse but the look of terror on their faces was priceless. Certainly mine was when they did it to me as an initiation.

Unlike the UK at the time, the horses were turned out as much as possible. Which was fine, except that there weren't many head-collars in the yard. Horses were taken straight to the fields from their work and all turned out together. Mares were separate, but very few. When it was time to get them in, a length of baler twine would suffice, or two horses at once, if you were lucky to be in possession of two lengths of twine!

The autumn of 1988 was relatively dry. The horses were turned out without rugs daily. As winter approached, the rain started, and particularly muddy horses became the norm. I, being English and naive, asked one of the lads, called Dotty, if we should perhaps groom the horses. He replied, 'Why?! Arthur'll only torn'em out agen t'morrow!' Hence, I learned that horses, indeed animals, don't care what they look like. As long as they are warm, fed and watered they are happier to be filthy from their freedom each day.

It was a big job with so many horses and so many young lads, many away from home for the first time. Training the lads was a massive part of my job...or maybe they trained me....

Arthur always had a waiting list of potential staff: as soon as one left, usually after we had trained him, another greenhorn would arrive to be educated. I will always remember a new lad arriving from Co. Galway. I asked, 'What's your background in Galway, James?'

'We are farmers,' he replied.

'What do you grow?'

'Potatoes. Barley. Turnips. Wheat. Grass.'

'You must be a big farm?'

'Yes, 45 acres!'

I was yet to experience the West of Ireland, it seems.

Sunday mornings at Dereens meant a 10am start. This supposedly was to give all the staff a chance to go to Mass before work. It seemed reasonable enough to me. However, I soon learned that Mass could also be attended on Saturday night, so any of the lads could go to Saturday evening Mass wearing their best togs and then go straight out on the lash afterwards.

Confessions Of A Slow Two-Miler

A 10am Sunday start meant that usually we had a full complement of Sunday staff. Any earlier would have been a struggle for some of them.

We had some very fine riders, and it helped that we were all young and fearless. Having said that, the vast majority of rides were easy enough and most of the horses were well broken and sensible. An exception was Dick the Spuddler.

He was a bay horse by Furry Glen. He was perhaps the most runaway horse I've ever had anything to do with! Luckily the circular gallops there were enclosed and you just rode the horse round and round until it bottomed itself or decided to stop. It was planned that its first run would be at a maiden point-to-point in Summerhill, in 1990. It was a Sunday and I recall that the Saturday night had been particularly messy. We arrived at the County Meath track and met the owners' representative who, let's say, enjoyed a drink. Somehow I got the horse to the start, which was no mean feat I can tell you! The race set off with me not very confident at all.

The fences in the race were the metal portable type, and the further we went the lower the horse was getting over the jumps, until his shoes were clanking on the metal frames. I was upsides a pal called David Geoghegan, and I turned to him and said, 'This is going to fall!' CRASH. I've never been so relieved to get off a horse.

Back in the paddock, the owner's representative was gushing with praise: 'Mattchew, Mattchew, Mattchew, that ride, you gave it a hell of a ride, a great ride! You were surely going to win!' (Yeah, right!!) He pulled out some notes for me and it revealed as 150 punts worth! Thank you very much!

The rest of the day descended into point-to-point car boot type parties. At the end of the afternoon, there were not many cars left. A random gentleman was spotted going into a portaloo near to his own car boot celebrations. Conor O'Dwyer, standing with us, perked up as he saw an opportunity arise. 'Jeez, wouldn't it be funny if we pushed that toilet over with him still inside?' And he started running.

Three jockeys, prompted by his actions, duly raced off too. Conor soon stopped, and I had remained static. The others pushed the cubicle over onto its door, with the hapless racegoer trapped within. The hoots of laughter were heard by all as the fellas ran back to our car. The unfortunate's wife, who was heavily pregnant, demanded help to extract her husband from the smelly coffin. We returned to the crime scene to assist the soggy gentleman, and although details following this event are hazy to my memory, I seem to

Team Moore - *courtesy of Caroline Norris*

remember us all drinking in the local pub a bit later, sewage-victim included. I also remember in the same pub bumping into the very drunken owner's representative who once again unleashed his stream of praise. 'I mean it was just a great ride, great ride, you were going to win for sure!! For sure! And, did I pay you yet?? I can't remember....' I don't think I answered either way, and he duly cashed his cheque at the bar and gave me another 150 punts! To be fair, for the type of horse it was and the daily work I was exposed to on it, a bit of extra danger-money felt quite deserved!

The soiled gentleman subsequently identified his portaloo pushers and learnt that one of them was considered racing royalty and took legal action for damages. It was settled out of court.

After racing on one Sunday in March, I schooled a young horse round Navan. As standard, I had no idea what plan Arthur had been hatching. It emerged after the schooling that the horse had been entered for a point-to-point the following weekend at Gowran Park. Arthur let me know I was expected to ride it, and I duly went to work early on Sunday morning to complete the work before heading to the races. I arrived to discover the owner's groom had come to collect the horse, and the owner intended to lead the horse up himself, rather than the usual lad-and-transport arrangements. Alarm bells started ringing! There must be a punt on! However, the previous weekend, I had flown to the UK to ride a hunter chase winner at Doncaster, which was noted and commented on in the gossip column of the Irish Field: 'Arthur Moore's assistant Matt Sheppard rode a winner at Doncaster.' So instead of being some Young Buck, all of a sudden, I'd gained a little bit of a profile. Any chances of an Under the Radar gentleman amateur rider Matt Sheppard were quashed.

I rocked up at Gowran Park, and the owner was down in the race card as the trainer. I was handed the colours: a black and yellow hooped rugby jersey, and a Pony Club type elastic black hat silk. I weighed out and handed the saddle over. When I met the owner in the paddock, the horse was being led round with straw in its tail, a lead rope made from a grubby broken lunge-line, and the horse was covered in a ropey sweat sheet. 'Mm,' I thought, 'Trying to keep things under cover?'

Circling around down at the start I struck up conversation with top English point-to-point rider Simon Andrews. He was on an away day with a random book of rides sorted by some enthusiastic connection. He said, 'Hey Matt, do you know anything about who trains this horse that I am riding?'

Chapter 4

'Should jump OK,' I replied.

'Well,' said Simon, 'You would hope that they would have some good rubber reins on the bridle!' I glanced at his tack and observed that his reins were bare leather and any of the normal rubber grip had been worn away, which would give any jockey riding an unknown horse more than a little cause for concern!

However, in the race everything went well for me and my ride, until approaching two out. We were travelling well, looking a likely winner, but we over-jumped and sprawled on landing. We hadn't fooled anyone, though. The Irish Field reported that 'Out Of Court, ridden by Matt Sheppard and trained by Arthur Moore would definitely have won had they not fallen at the second-last.' The horse did prove to be quite good.

The owner was a Dublin lawyer. Once he turned up at the yard during evening stables. I had been clipping a difficult horse and had been kicked in the knee, and was upside-down in the corner of the clipping box. The lawyer-owner popped his head in the box, saw my distress and said, 'Whose horse kicked you, shall we sue?'

'That would be great,' I grunted, 'It was yours!' He disappeared very quickly.

***

I am a great believer that everything should happen to one at least once in your life! For example, being sued, meeting certain people or having various unmissable experiences. I have to confess being interviewed for murder is not a normal experience for most people.

One Sunday morning in September 1990 a bookmaker called Des Fox was stopped, robbed and shot in the legs on his way to the Curragh races. He tragically bled to death! The gangsters escaped in a red car down the bog road past Dereen's stables where I also had a red car. To help with their enquiries, the Gardai needed to track my movements and eliminate me and my motor from the scene. There was no CCTV in those days and the bog road was a very rural one. A wizened detective with a gnarly look from a classic crime drama took my statement and I was happy to help. Several months later we bumped into the detective in The Manor pub and I asked him about progress. He said that they knew exactly who was responsible but didn't have enough to prosecute. In 2018 two men were arrested but released without charge.

Working for Arthur took a lot of mind-reading! In the late 80s there was a very popular sire called Furry Glen. All his offspring seemed to be a nice stamp, Arthur's typical favourite specimen. At one time there must have been at seven young Furry Glen geldings out of 65 horses in the yard.

Arthur's handwritten morning work list was always written in code that took a lot of deciphering. Hence we had Big FG, Little FG, JW FG (Jack Whites), 3yo FG, Bay FG (they were all bay). Following a request once to pull out and trot up 'the Furry Glen', I asked which one he needed and Arthur barked, 'the fucking bay one.'

All the young horses were labelled by their sire until named, and even then their names were secret until they had race entries made for them. On one occasion there was a horse due to have a hobday wind operation. 'Matt, please go and catch the 'so and so' from the field and load it onto the trailer ready to go to the vets for surgery!' As my mind reading skills were not highly trained at this stage of my Irish adventure I asked, 'Which horse is that?'

'The one with the headcollar.'

There was only one gelding in the field wearing a headcollar, and yard headcollars were a rare commodity. What could go wrong? I duly caught said horse and loaded it onto the trailer. Arthur took the horse to the vets himself and returned to the yard. On passing the field he spotted what must have been the horse intended for the surgery, not wearing a headcollar. He went into meltdown and dashed up to the house to use the nearest phone, to stop the surgery. Too late! The vet, Ned Gowing, covered himself by saying that a pre-operation endoscopic examination of the horse revealed that it needed a hobday anyway.

My time in Ireland was fairly low key. At that time in the depths of winter there were few midweek fixtures, and two meetings on one day were unheard of. So my days at the racecourse were rare unless it was my day off. In a big UK yard my job would have involved lots of days racing at the second meeting and representing the trainer dealing with that day's owners. Owners turning up at Dereens, and therefore ever meeting them, was a very rare occurrence. I did, however, meet JP McManus one day when he showed up to view a horse that was for sale.

Arthur had a very good system. Every year he sourced and bought ten foals, either privately or at auction. He had a top secret system which revolved around how many sires in the pedigree had sired a certain number of stakes winners in a past rolling five years. So all the sires would have a tally of

Chapter 4

progeny successes and a young horse with a certain total would qualify for at least an inspection. A few other factors would kick in like its conformation, the dam's pedigree, whether any young relatives were improving types, and finally the 'dollar', his perception of its value. What tended to happen with these plans is that one year's draft can be very successful and a real good money earner with a nice profit margin, but the following year's draft purchased with exactly the same criteria could be very moderate. But life is like that and we are dealing with animals. A sire's popularity can change overnight. There is no doubt that you can make mistakes which are a disaster and mistakes which turn out to be money earners. And some purchases would be a horsemanship hunch.

So each season there would be at least ten youngsters coming through the system. Ready to be broken in, semi-trained, turned away and being aimed to run in their four-year-old season if not too backward or beset with problems. Some years you may have four out of ten potential superstars or horses you could sell for big money and some years you could end up with a big fat zero of potential!

My first winter at Dereens was fairly grim. The yard had a virus and it made for a trying time for the boss and a lot of disappointing days. This was before there was televised racing in betting shops, so watching our horses run was not possible except for Saturday on RTE. So reports of performance either came from Arthur, in his usual code form; or Tom Taaffe, who was always flexible with the truth in case there was potential for a gamble – unless he knew something that the rest of us didn't – but in general none of us really knew what was going on.

My second season at Dereens was a real buzz, the yard rocked along and some really good horses emerged and in my third season Arthur topped the trainers' table. At the time I didn't realise the enormity of the achievement, but looking back it was huge. It was the last time an old-fashioned traditional type of yard won the title; subsequent winners are a new breed and it is sad that those days have gone. The attention to detail these days is second to none and veterinary science has removed a great deal of horsemanship.

In training at Dereens were mainly geldings, but there was one particular filly that tested everyone. She was a juvenile three-year-old filly and Madam was her middle name. She had begun to be reluctant to enter the starting stalls on the flat, so needed to switch codes. When she first arrived she wouldn't even enter through a stable door so we constructed an enclosure of round hay bales in the barn and rolled them into position around her when she returned from the paddock after exercise. Arthur would chase her around the gallop in the van banging the driver's door, blasting the horn and yelling loudly. At the time there was a fictional drama on TV called *Trainer* and the principal character had a horse to train with a similar attitude, so he resorted to chasing the unwilling beast in his vehicle playing a ghetto blaster loudly behind the horse to make it gallop quicker and make it fit enough to race. For any younger readers: a ghetto blaster was an enormous set of portable speakers for youths to play loud music back in the 1980s. Arthur clearly hadn't watched the programme because when one of the lads suggested that the boss try the same trick Arthur replied, 'What the fucking hell is a ghetto blaster?'

The mare did have some ability and was worth persevering with. At Punchestown the horses were down at the start and our jockey had organised for one of the ground staff to cut two short lengths of gorse which he was able to prickle each side of her withers to keep her on her toes and not thinking about avoiding lining up at the tapes. Imagine the outrage today if TV cameras picked up such 'abject cruelty': the anti-brigade would make a right meal out of it.

Arthur paid the lads' weekly wages in old used envelopes and during one summer when Mary and he were away, I was instructed to visit the AIB bank in Newbridge on Friday afternoon to collected the prepared wage packets. The bank staff had no knowledge of such a collection, so I returned to Dereens with no cash to pay the lads' wages. I was convinced that the youngest Moore, Andrew, had the wages secreted away with instruction not to release the envelopes with an 'only codding you' moment at 5.55pm on Friday. Poor lad, I gave him a really hard time (he was only about ten years old), but no wages were forthcoming. Eventually with no contact from Arthur, Mrs Jones, who was Mary Moore's mother, wrote a cheque for 500 punts which big Jim Sheridan took to his night job of head barman in a bar in Naas. When takings were sufficient, he cashed Mrs Jones's cheque and on Saturday morning I was at least able to give the boys some Saturday night beer money. The prepared wages at the bank eventually emerged having been handled by a part time bank worker and got lost in the system. The very apologetic

Chapter 4

manager even offered me a good mortgage deal as compensation for the bank's failings.

One bright late spring/early summer Monday morning a minibus pulled up outside the yard full of young people accompanied by some lecturers. This was a familiar sight from my agricultural college days. The driver jumped out and announced that they were on a Warwickshire College of Agricultural Equine Studies course, and they had come for a stable visit. It was news to me and Arthur was not around and his wife Mary had no idea of the appointment. Luckily I knew what was expected, because of my student days, but my heart sank because I knew that word had got out that Arthur was not going to be present in the morning and as a result Sunday stables were devoid of any mucking out: the yard was a bombsite. To top it off, a load of lads turned up hungover and late. I motivated the team into action and took the visitors on a tour of the gallops and all the fields of youngstock at Dereens. By the time we arrived back at the yard, the lads had shaped up and I gave a tour round the horses in training at the time. I quite enjoyed it! I think it went down well with the students. Right at the end I asked if anyone had any questions. A young girl put her hand up to ask, 'What qualifications do you have for your job?' She was deflated at my answer of 'Absolutely zero!'

I had some great days at the Irish point-to-points. On one occasion THE Aidan O'Brien asked to use my weight cloth to double weigh at a Cashel meet. It was a heavy duty, strong cloth, able to carry the great deal of lead weights needed for a lightweight jockey to make the weight up to twelve stone. It is a great claim to fame to tell all the budding young jockeys who have also borrowed it in recent years. Conversely – a legendary Irish champion point-to-point jockey who didn't need a weight cloth in the latter years of his career was Enda Bolger. At a point-to-point meeting in the late 1980s came an announcement over the tannoy, 'Enda Bolger will carry twelve stone four pounds in all races!'

On a Sunday in April 1992 three young maiden horses were loaded on to a lorry to run in a point-to-point in Castletown Geoghegan. It became clear that Arthur wasn't going to be attending, which was not normal and there was a certain sense that we were going to wing it. The plan was to declare three horses for one maiden race and rely on it being divided on the day. I was to ride one in each division and Humphrey Murphy the other one. Near to declaration deadline time it was becoming apparent that the

21 declarations needed for the race to divide wasn't going to happen. Jim Errity, a pal of Arthur's who was declarations clerk, said, 'Don't worry Matt, I'll sort it,' and deliberately miscounted the number of declarations and set about dividing the race appropriately. Until a sharp-eyed steward spotted the error. Bugger! A twenty-runner maiden with every single jockey on the track engaged to ride. One owner was on track, so I decided to ride his mount, Humphrey rode his designated mount, which left the most fancied runner needing a rider. There was no mobile communication back then, so step up Jim Murphy. Dereens' feed man had never ridden in a race before – he didn't even school horses at home – but he did have his kit. Anyhow, it was a complete non-event. I pulled up, Humphrey pulled up and Jim fell. The horses were all fine. We loaded and sent them back on the lorry. I followed them home and arrived back 30 minutes later and sheepishly reported to Arthur our crap day. Jim had briefly summed up events (pu, pu, fell) without any elaboration. Jim was carrying a broken collarbone without a whinge and didn't tell Arthur that he had piloted the most fancied runner. My review of the day to Arthur went down better than expected and my reflection in hindsight is that he knew that all the horses were all useless and whatever happened would make no difference to their value or prospects.

After many divisions of races at a Fairyhouse point-to-point dusk was drawing in with one race left to run. I didn't have a mount in this one. The stewards asked the jockeys if they were happy to ride, which of course they were. Following the race with very little commentary there were multiple loose horses tearing about and officials were in their vehicles, headlights on, checking for fallen jockeys on the landing side of all the fences.

I did manage to ride an Irish point to point winner for Arthur at Roscommon in April 1991, but my race riding in Ireland was pretty underwhelming. Having said that, I did have a few hurdle spins round Punchestown, including riding against Tommy Carmody on one occasion, which I suppose illustrates how once again a sport like horse racing which can seem elite and exclusive to the average person, can actually be quite inclusive.

At Leopardstown for a Sunday midwinter meeting, by the time we had staggered out of the bar and found our car in the car park we were surprised to find a very drunken woman spread-eagled face down across the bonnet. To describe her as mutton would be a discredit to old sheep, more like a broken mouthed scraggy mountain ewe on her last mission to escape from her last pen. Her pencil thin legs were sticking out from a short velvety shirt with a

Chapter 4

leopard skin jacket and she had a black hat that looked like a currant on her head. With plenty of dangly jewellery and high heels, she must have been freezing. Fairly merry ourselves, we offered our gentlemanly services to the non-damsel in distress. 'Can we help you, madam?' She turned over and sat her backside on the bonnet. 'I can't find my car,' she squawked, 'It's a red Datsun.' We retrieved her keys and started a search. It was late and there were not many cars left, so we thought 'it can't be that difficult.' But it was dark and there was no flashing light central locking back in those days. A red Datsun was not obvious anywhere in the near vicinity and it transpired she was in wrong car park! Dave Geoghegan, who was with us, started trying the key in other random car doors and eventually opened a white Nissan. He jumped in, turned the key in the ignition and bingo it started. Dave bundled her in protesting that 'this is not my car' and she kangarooed off telling us she was going to the on-site Gardai station to 'tell them what she had done.' Meanwhile we jumped in our car and used her as a distraction for the Gardai as we hightailed it out of another exit.

As usual Arthur kept his plans secret and caught me out on a Saturday morning when I rocked up to work to be informed that I was riding that afternoon in a handicap hurdle at Punchestown. It presented two issues. Firstly, I had been on a Friday night out in Naas where too much drink was consumed, and secondly I was due to pick up Nicky from Dublin airport mid-afternoon. There were no mobile phones back then but I manged to contact my then housemate Joe O'Flynn to collect Nicky. Neither knew what each other looked like so he managed to get the airport tannoy to ask 'will the lady who is meeting Matt Sheppard please go to the meeting point.'

Joe O'Flynn's family ran a very exclusive country house hotel called Rathsallagh and they were kind enough to invite me for Christmas lunch. I arrived and entered through the back kitchen and saw that the food preparation was going well. I did notice a dressed turkey on the side but thought maybe it was for later in the week. In the living room we started on an endless supply of champagne. A couple of hours passed and Joe's mother Kay suddenly remembered that she hadn't put the turkey in the oven! It was a very long messy afternoon before we ate our Christmas meal.

During my gap year in New Zealand my pal Glyn and I met an English back packer called Mark Hill. We exchanged some banter over some beer and probably thought 'nice bloke but we will never meet him again'. However, on the final six weeks of our tour when we were sightseeing round the North

Island, we picked him up hitch-hiking in some remote location. More beer and banter. 'Bye, have a good life.' Six years later I am sharing a house in Naas with Joe and the phone rings and a fella asks to speak to Joe, who wasn't at home and leaves a message, 'Tell him Mark Hill rang.' I put the phone down and thought that voice and name sounded familiar. Later Joe produced a photo of them together on a skiing holiday and it was the same Mark Hill. I met him again when he came to Ireland for the New Year and thought that was farewell. Two years later, when Nicky and I were working in Wiltshire I bumped into him again in a pub in Sherston. I don't really know Mark but have a funny feeling he is the sort of guy I may meet again randomly!

***

Liam Cusack was a jump jockey in Ireland at the time and was struggling with his weight. He was in conversation with his then boss, the very successful businessman-cum-trainer Jim Bolger, who sternly told him that 'eating and drinking is only a habit.'

CHAPTER 5

THE ONLY WAY IS EASTNOR

I finished at Arthur's in 1992. Nicky, who had been working for Jessie Harrington, was keen to return home and although we were having a great time in Ireland, living in a semi-derelict squat on a pittance of a wage was beginning to wear thin. I answered an advertisement in the *Sporting Life* for an assistant trainer and was offered a job by Martyn Meade, who I knew from riding point-to-point winners back in 1986. The money offered was good and the living accommodation was much superior to our existing hovel, so with a heavy heart, I left Dereens. Although I very quickly regretted my move, if I hadn't moved then I would not have had the life that I have had since. The new job at Sherston was quite successful for training winners but it wasn't a happy ship to be aboard, so we parted company after one season.

When Nicky and I married in 1993 we inherited some point-to-point owners from Nicky's mother, Jackie. Eastnor Estate in Herefordshire was keen to diversify, and encourage new blood and business into the village. With the aid of their land agent Robert Killen we moved into Home Farm, where we still live now. In July we moved into the cottage with absolutely fuck all! It had no carpets, no kitchen, no lightbulbs; nothing. We raided a skip to source some carpets. The furniture was all second-hand and the only heating was a burnt-out Rayburn.

The yard outside was mud, mud and more mud, but although there were only three stables at that time, there were barns with potential for more stabling. The upside of the deal was, and still is, very cheap rent. And although we made improvements ourselves at our own expense, in the long run our rent reviews could only go up a small percentage each time, and made the process affordable. Not borrowing any money from the bank is the main reason why we have managed to stay in business.

The other upside was that it was an undiscovered gem of a location to train racehorses. The old turf hills were a joy to discover. I couldn't believe that no one had trained here before us.

In the first year at Eastnor I managed to land a shift-work job at Sun Valley chicken factory at Yazor Road in Hereford. On a permanent 2pm until 10pm shift, I worked all morning on the yard with any horses we could attract before working eight hours making turkey sausages! Earning a weekly wage provided funds to buy breeze blocks and we built stables as horses arrived. It was a job. It was a means to an end. There were people working in the factory who were resigned to this existence for the rest of their working lives, with their partners working in other parts of the factory too.

There were also people like me, with small businesses, striving to make their lives better. Other smallholders had bought their own land and struggled to pay the mortgage with their farm income alone. So a five-day week shift work at the factory provided them with regular money: half a day to work on their farm, half in the factory, and they would take their annual leave at lambing time. Another extraordinary co-worker was Tommy Philby, the son of notorious spy Kim Philby. I had met Tommy as he was a point to point jockey in the area, but it seemed quite surreal that he should end up working in such a lowly place.

I'm not sure I would get away with it now, but on a couple of occasions I started my afternoon shift in the factory, bunked off to Ludlow racecourse to ride in the hunter chase, then back to Yazor Road to finish the shift. My time at the factory came to an end when I switched shifts to ride at a midweek point-to-point fixture at Eyton-on-Severn. My co-worker on the turkey sausage production line agreed to swap with me. Instead of my planned 2pm until 10pm shift, I worked from 6am until 2pm, drove straight to the fixture, fell at the last when in second, got knocked unconscious, and was ambulanced to Shrewsbury Hospital to spend three days in a daze before being released.

I never returned to the factory; the yard got busy. I recovered from the fall but that proved to be my last race ride. Additionally, our landlords appointed us jobs as caravan park wardens for the deer park touring site. A Land Rover was supplied and we had a daily job collecting the fees from the visiting caravans, which fitted in well with the rest of our business. The Land Rover came in very useful, as up until then any visiting point-to-point owners who didn't drive a 4x4 were required to walk to the top of the gallop, which is no mean feat in itself. Furthermore, on some occasions it was raining and blowing a gale, and the visitors wearing townie-type country clothes found it an experience that they did not want to repeat!

There was a mountain bike racing event in the deer park in the summer of 1995 and as a result of too much drinking and too much sun the event became very rowdy and a near riot ensued. In the melée a teenager was stabbed to

Chapter 5

death. On the Sunday morning I drove down to check on the campers and saw multiple policemen and long queues of cars exiting and made some enquiries as to what was going on. On learning of the tragic night, I reported back to my landlord at the castle (who was completely unaware of any incident) who proclaimed that it was 'great publicity for Eastnor.'

CHAPTER 6

THE GOLDEN AGE OF POINT-TO-POINTS

My very earliest memory as a child, is being at the Larkhill Point-to-Point, when I must have been about three or four years old. I didn't take much notice of the racing. My father was riding, but I was playing with some friends in a couple of burned-out tanks which were abandoned nearby (Larkhill is a military base). My second early point-to-point memory is attending the Mendip Hunt meeting at Nedge and witnessing a one-armed jockey competing. He was well-mounted on a reliable type of steed and I was informed that the other jockeys rode on his outside around the bends to help keep his horse on track. I am fairly sure that the authorities would not be very happy to accommodate such an intrepid cavalier in this day and age.

The UK point-to-point scene has been a bastion of rural life. The local hunt would run a meeting at the end of the hunting season, to test the hunt horses, who would compete in a three mile steeplechase, and they would supply some hospitality and sport for the landowners whose land had been crossed in the season's hunting. Many of the farmers were hunters with point-to-pointers themselves. The season started in early February and went on until June. Meetings were on Saturdays and Bank Holidays, even sometimes midweek, notably the Heythrop and Croome & West Warwick fixture on Easter Tuesday. Race planning was basic, with simple rules of administration.

The Golden Age of point-to-pointing was in the 1980s and 90s. One of the biggest changes was the introduction of Sunday racing. Before that moment, the point-to-point community was very tight-knit. After a busy Saturday with meetings staged up and down the country, all the local trainers and jockeys would collect in the local pubs, and exchange accounts of how their days had fared, and catch up on other meetings gossip and results. There was no racing the next day, so a long night in the pub was the norm. In recent times, the internet provides all the results, and busy Sundays encourage less people to have a late night.

Before emails and online banking, owners and trainers would have to post entries two weeks before, with a certain entry received by the Saturday before the race to ensure a place.

Chapter 6

Due to many variables around racing, mainly weather, multiple entries would be made for each horse, resulting in many decisions to be made about where to run on Saturday mornings. Maybe your desired jockey could not commit, or maybe the ground was unsuitable following overnight rain, or lack of it. In my early days riding it wasn't unusual to pick up a really good spare on the day.

With mobile phones, multiple weekend fixtures, a declining population of point-to-pointers and resulting smaller fields, jockeys can now dictate where they want to ride, and good horses avoid each other. The result is a lot of uncompetitive contests.

The old boys tell of the good Open horses taking each other on every week, and depending on the track: a long three miles, or short three; a galloping track or a sharper one; certain super-star horses could have a large following, with locals turning up every week to cheer on their favourites. Alas, progress has led to decline.

Unlicensed trainers and owners are having an awesome sport put on for then by hard-working Point-to-Point Committees. But nowadays, the people who go hunting don't go point-to- pointing, and the people who go point-to-pointing don't go hunting. There are also a lot less traditional rural-type folk. Farms are bigger and more mechanised, so there are fewer farm-workers, many of which are now European with no interest in country sports. And there are multiple sports televised which allow point-to-pointing to be out-competed. A 60-inch TV in a warm, comfy lounge is often perceived a better option to a cold and muddy field.

We started out our training business from the very bottom. We trained our first two winners on the same day. I rode an Eastnor-trained winner at Upton-upon-Severn on a grey mare called Knowing and Nicky rode another one at Barbury Castle on a horse owned by her mother called Deerfencer. Before mobile phones we didn't know of each other's success until we all returned home. The sport was in its heyday, every farmer had a horse, small syndicates were common, there were plenty of horses available and the fun element was epic. Horses like Upton Adventure, Cruise A Hoop, Lough Ennel, Up There, Strong Weld, were multiple winners and with champion rider Julian Pritchard on board we manged to win races with some very moderate horses because we had them very fit and ridden by the best rider.

We also had sporting owner-riders and the pre-season build up was electric. The game changed when Foot and Mouth closed down the countryside and many horses and connections diverted to National Hunt Rules. Many of these didn't return and some left altogether. The fact that it cost the same to keep a pointer in training to run for peanuts reward as it does to run under Rules for prize money is an issue as well as the fact that it is harder to win a point-to-point, as under Rules a very moderate animal with limited point-to-point potential can win prize money with a handicap mark.

One particular point-to-point training performance of note was a horse called Duke Of Spain. He was bred as the result of breeding from a gifted (as in free) mare to the cheapest available local stallion. He was an enormous beast with a complete mind of his own. When we were teaching him how to gallop, we had to pony him off another horse, gallop him on a lead rein and teach him to jump. This involved the jockey on the pony leading Duke in towards the schooling fence and passing over the lead rope to Duke's rider when he was lined up and got some speed up. Luckily, he was a good jumper so minimal schooling was necessary. I was schooling him myself over the baby jumps on one occasion and he was being very reluctant. Whatever happened, it was always unwise to strike him with your stick. I was riding in a general purpose saddle and in his temper he tried to rear, but it was more of a flip backwards. In such crisis moments the trusted way to escape any injury is to lean as far forward as possible and minimise contact with the horse's mouth by having very slack rein contact. Duke flipped, had all four limbs off the ground, I was upright and parallel with the horse's spine, chin between his ears with my stirrup leathers parallel with my shin and my feet nearly touching the grass either side of his tail, at which point the leathers slipped off the bars which attach them to the saddle and I was left standing whilst the horse flipped himself back on to four legs. I safely survived a very tricky moment. He had heaps of ability but only consented to win one maiden race and even then tried to pull himself up passing the horsebox park.

We were sent Strong Weld by the owner-breeders who had just moved in to the area. He had won a modest maiden on rock hard ground and after a few runs on soft going he used to pulverise modest opposition making all the running with fast accurate jumping on quick ground. He loved jumping. We were using him as lead schooling horse one day and he was being ridden by Abi, who was having her first go at schooling over fences. We have a line of three fences, two sections wide and well-winged but with no pilot there is plenty of room for a horse to run out. Without Strong Weld making any mistake Abi fell off and the horse attacked the other two fences solo, which very few horses would have attempted. The horse liked to jump off a long stride and I was stood by a fence at Hackwood Park and witnessed him putting in a short stride before take-off in order to go long! The horse took us to Aintree and in a very competitive Foxhunters led a big field to the second last, jumping the big fences in spectacular fashion to finish a respectable ninth of 29. The owners ran out money and were losing interest so I recommended Rhys Jenkins to buy the horse. He did a deal which included an extra grand when he won a race on it. On his first spin at Howick Point-to-Point the new pairing won a two horse race by two fences. Rhys and the horse had a glorious second season winning five races and nine in total. Overall, he won fourteen points and a novice chase while trained at Eastnor.

***

'I had to go on a mission to collect a considerable amount of unpaid training fees that had very slow in being paid. On broaching the subject with the owner's wife, she burst into tears and wailed, 'How am I going to pay the school fees?'

Upton Adventure, Emma James, multiple winner at Garnons point-to-point.

CHAPTER 7

MATT SHEPPARD: RACEHORSE TRAINER

My job description is 'Racehorse Trainer', because 'Miracle Worker' doesn't feature anywhere in a dropdown menu box on any online form – but then again, neither does racehorse trainer. I suppose, because there are less than 600 hundred trainers in the UK at any one time, I am in a very privileged minority of people whose hobby is also my job. A good day in this job is second to none. The winning owners' faces; being greeted into the winners' enclosure to cheers and claps; meeting the great and the good alongside the gamblers and lowlifes; comparing stories, win lose or draw.

There are lots of disappointing days, but a really bad day is travelling home with a badly injured horse, or worse an empty horse box, or even worse, knowing that a jockey has been stretchered off and we are waiting for a good news bulletin.

When working with athletic animals, every day is a school day. Most of them have some quirks or characteristic which make them individuals. With our yard and system, many horses spend their entire racing careers at Eastnor. And because we are very hands-on and spend plenty of time with each horse, we don't miss much. In bigger yards, where numbers are larger and time is scarcer, individuals may get overlooked by a more factory type approach at producing horses. Lots of different staff may ride any one horse day-on-day, which makes it harder to know if something is off colour. In Eastnor, the partnerships are mostly fixed and each staff member really 'knows' their horse. Being a small yard we are risking horses that we can't afford to lose or go wrong and forego valuable income, so they are worth looking after very carefully.

When I get bad news about a horse and a career-ending injury, or you lose one to a racecourse fatality, the first thing to go through my mind is, 'Fuck; that's one less payer.' A sad thought, I know, as is, 'Is it going to be replaced?' There is no guaranteed income in this game and that one monthly fee is the difference between breaking even or making a loss and when your numbers are limited it is impossible to absorb the ongoing expenses. For us it is easier to make a loss because there are fewer horses and every time you gallop is a risk, let alone putting them under race conditions.

Let me describe the daily routine.

Chapter 7

When the core season is up and running, a usual day starts at 6am with a feed and I feel the horses' legs for heat, swelling, but mainly changes. I think it is important to feel the legs at the same time every day, otherwise harmless fluctuations in body temperature and fluid retention may mislead. First thing in the morning is the most consistent time. Then it's into the office with coffee, switch on the laptop and catch up on possible entries and declarations. I take Mrs Shep a 7am coffee with a quick chat about the morning work list, then the staff begin turning up for a 7.30am start.

The first lot pulls out 7.45am and we always leave a member of staff in the yard to muck out the empty boxes whilst they are vacant, so as not to shake up bedding and create unnecessary dust for horses to inhale. Racehorse lungs are sensitive and crucial in the realms of their purpose, and anyone who has mucked out and then blown their nose will know how dusty a business it is!

The horses come back from exercise and in recent years we have changed our policy of using a hose-pipe to wash them off unless absolutely necessary, as this only encourages skin conditions like mud fever. Instead we use the stable rubbers/towels which are used between a horse's back and the saddle pad to rub and dry any sweaty patches on the girth or saddle areas. We then rug them up with turn-out rugs and let them dig and roll in their wallows and they come in filthy but happy. In midwinter especially, when the paddocks may be very wet, we rub the legs dry, mainly under the fetlocks where long hair tends to let the cold water hang.

We never wash them off anymore and have had nowhere near as much mud fever since that decision. Science has revealed it is more dependent on temperature rather than the presence of mud itself, so soaking the skin with cold water allows the organism found in the mud to penetrate more successfully. Nonetheless, we have to be alert to a sensitive horse, chestnuts and those with white legs.

The horses may spend an hour or two out with each other (mares and geldings separate). We run the risk of one getting kicked and injured, but the benefits of down time just Being Horses for them is a big bonus. As always there is always a day when you regret a turn out moment. On one occasion just before Cheltenham Seek The Faith received a kick to a hind leg below the hock and fractured a splint bone (which in some ways is good because bone injuries heal better than a tendon or ligament injury) but it set us back and the horse missed his intended run at the Festival. To be fair it was probably a good thing because the owner, as usual, had an unrealistic target. The other bonus is that giving the horses the opportunity to roll outside in a field they rarely try to roll in their stables which can be hazardous.

Before a race day the intended runner will get a hot bath and shampoo ready for the next day's outing. On a race day in midwinter a very early start can be in order, depending on how far away the meeting is. We like to be on course two hours before the race. If it is local, and maybe involving a fretful horse, you might try and get to the course at the very last minute, with 45 minutes before the race being the rule.

I learned a long time ago that for me, having young horses and trying to win novice races wasn't ever going to be a successful or sustainable way of performing. I never had the money to buy the correct type of young horse with enough ability. That's not to say we never won some novice hurdles with some horses that we were sent, or that I declined an owner who specifically wanted me to find them a young horse. The main thing is that we go down the other route of buying second-hand, handicapped, maybe jaded horses that could be rejuvenated or as we say, 'Eastnored.'

We do this without a fixed gallop in sight. Lots of grassy hills, woods and banks to get horses fit with maximum lung and heart exercise and minimum strain on legs. The horses we mostly get sent already know how to gallop, and if you can get them fit without them realising then you stand a chance of getting them back to some form. It doesn't happen every time. I have taken a chance on plenty without success but it is very satisfying when it does.

Another reason – other than financial – that young horses weren't the sphere I pursued was the shortage these days of young rough-riding lads. Realistic, rather than sexist: young boys just don't get scared like girl riders. The shortage of such lads is due to the change in the amount of true country families. Thirty years ago, there were lots of hunting farmers with sons and daughters brought up in the hunt pony clubs. They had lots of stockmanship and horsemanship about them, loads of practicality, and lots of them had no fear! But as the farms have got bigger and farmers have got fewer, and the shooting farmers have overtaken the hunting farmers, so there are less and less young people coming through with the desire to be jockeys or point-to-point riders.

There is a whole generation now of 'riding club' type riders who aren't quite up to the mark to ride thoroughbreds. Most of the good lads want to be jockeys and my set up is unable to give them the opportunities they need to even get on to slippery jockey ladder. Small family yards are finding it

Chapter 7

a constant struggle to attract good enough staff. In Eire, the powerhouses of Elliott, Mullins and the O'Brien family mop up all the top staff with top wages and conditions.

However, at Eastnor the aforementioned variety of hills help to get the right amount and quality of work into the horses without necessarily needing the best of riders. If a horse starts at the bottom of a hill and gets to the top with a passenger aboard, it has had a good blow and done a piece of work.

Horses are animals, but you can't beat a horse that will try its best for you. They make it easier to train, easier to find races for, and easier to win races with. But sadly, very often the horses that try the hardest and keep going even if something is hurting, are the ones that go wrong. Some good horses can also have a dubious, doggy work ethic. These will actually last a long time and will probably run well within their ability. They will be placed and win races and have a handicap mark, and because they are running with self-preservation, they can be expected to have a long racing career. But a good horse that tries really hard sometimes doesn't last very long, because they will get put up in class and in the handicap and they'll keep trying right until the end of their careers. Plenty of horses will try their hardest when they are young, and they will become jaded and become more reserved in their running as they get older, and to be honest you can't really blame them.

When starting out as a young new trainer you can very often be trying so hard that it in the long run, it does you more harm than good. You worry that that horses might be too fat and considered to be unfit and then if you have them too fit you are accused of having them too thin.

You must never worry what people think. When we were point-to-pointing in the early days the local pointing maestro had a reputation of working his horse really hard but also would present them at races looking in magnificent shape and winning regularly. His horses rarely ran under Rules and also stayed on the lorry when the dope wagon rocked up, blaming the ground for not running. 'The Master Feeder' was the general story. All the other trainers would try their best to compete but all were fighting a losing battle. His horses would look amazing and all ours would look like greyhounds!

Over the years we were sent two horses from that particular yard by owners looking to try under Rules, on both occasions the point-to-point trainer kept them for as long as possible to allow for any illegal substance to secrete from their system. One horse in particular arrived at Eastnor looking spectacular but after two reasonable placed runs the juice wore off

Confessions Of A Slow Two-Miler

and the poor horse melted into a sorry looking specimen of a hat rack and any ability he had vanished. Of course we were accused of being unable to feed a thoroughbred properly.

I never realised how powerful steroids were until I watched a friend die of cancer. Until the last three weeks of his life the steroids made him eat and kept weight on him. So much so that unless you knew he was ill you wouldn't have guessed.

All the trainers operating within the rules were on a hiding to nothing and it is still a common post-race pub conversation that really makes me mad. That the older racing faces didn't wake up, smell the coffee and cotton on as to what was going on instead of comparing us to a cheat. There, I said it. What everyone thought but no one would utter.

In business, to make a living it is not what you spend it is what you don't spend. A common mistake, made especially by young new faces starting out, is that they subsidise the owners' expenses, usually by providing cheap transport deals by doing it yourself. I did this right at the beginning, but soon learnt that to keep a lorry on the road, making it pay for itself, it needs to be on the road at least five days a week all year round. I am lucky if I have five runners a fortnight in mid-season so it proves to be a nice luxury to have horse transport provided by an outside contractor, who deals with all the legal stuff like a transport manager, operator's licence and drivers hours. Billing the owners for their services is a good way to focus some owners minds on exactly what makes up their costs. The same for vet's bills and farriers.

One particular mistake I made in the early days was trying to keep below the VAT threshold. This was mainly to keep the small owners on board with as little paperwork and administration as possible. To do this I made sure that every single extra was invoiced by the provider/supplier, and kept my daily fee to a minimum. This backfired when the size of my string ballooned and staff costs combined with a yard rent rise meant that an essential fee increase could only be a small percentage and nowhere near enough in the circumstances. It took more than a few years to scrape back up to making profit instead of just getting by.

A chap approached me wanting to send a horse that he had acquired. It was called Fortytwodee by a stallion called Amazing Bust. He had this idea that a bra manufacturing company would lease it and pay for it to be in training but until he sorted the details he wanted to pay me in bales of hay. He worked for the Highways Agency and baled hay cut from the side of the

Chapter 7

road. Mmmm. Thanks, but no thanks. I don't do deals and some polluted contaminated roadside fodder certainly didn't attract me. To his credit he secured a deal with Triumph Bras and Tony Carroll trained it to win a couple of small races.

There is a theory that there is a race in every horse. This is not true. But there are some owners and trainers who will persevere until the inevitable conclusion is made that it is useless. In point-to-pointing in particular, people will breed from a maggoty mare that won its only race at an Easter two-runner maiden on rock hard ground. They've then sent it to the cheapest stallion they could find locally, and guess what! Very occasionally they are successful. They take all the credit for the breeding plans; put their faith in the line that they have bred for generations; and how they Always Knew They Were Going to Breed a Winner.

A good example of this phenomenon is a point-to-pointer we trained for Peter Corbett called Upton Adventure. She was a black mare with a white face, a huge head and generally very poor conformation. She was from a long line of moderate horses. The stallion was called Green Adventure, a nomination prize won the previous season, out of the owner's previous Moderate Winning Mare.

We were sent two mares by Peter for breaking in, Rita and Mavis as they were nicknamed. Mavis was no trouble but Rita possessed a devilish pony streak and was a witch to break in. Mavis suffered all sorts of issues, mainly wind and sore shins. Rita, by contrast, was a machine. When we started working her, she could work with anything and was a very simple ride. When a young horse works as well as she did up our gallops, and have no pedigree, 99% of the time they are useless morning glories. But not Rita.

She had no character once she was broken in, a historical hock injury from when she fell off the ramp of a lorry. She was always resting that leg and many a time, after a good win, she would be resting it, and the next morning I would be convinced it had finally gone. But we would pull her out, she would take two maybe three lame strides but then be away, sound and without a bother. She would always go completely feral when turned out in the summer. Very often when we went to collect her the following autumn, we would take a team of staff to round her up from the enormous field she had holidayed in, into progressively smaller fields, then a cow yard, then a pen and eventually, when she was surrounded in a stable, she would give up.

On the racecourse she was a winning machine: 27 wins, and would have been more but the 2000 season was curtailed by Foot and Mouth. When she walked around the paddock, half asleep, some of the point-to-point crowd who may never have seen her before, must have viewed her and thought, 'WTF? Is that the so-called wonder mare?' And even Emma James, who rode her in Ladies races, confessed that for two miles in a three mile race she would feel like nothing special, until a slap down the shoulder, a 'yahoo' and she stepped up a gear to leave her rivals toiling. Her owner was a dedicated point to point follower, but if Rita had been campaigned under Rules she would have easily achieved a rating of 140 in two and three mile mares' races. Despite being completely devoid of breeding, conformation, character and fashion.

Molly Watson arrived on the scene to write a saucy fictional novel about hunting. She based it on the Ledbury Hunt along with all its characters and local goings-on. A nice young gentleman was in tow following Molly around like a lost puppy. At some point he decided that he would like to try riding in a point-to-point and sidled up to my wife out hunting for some advice. Nicky looked him up and down and advised that some weight loss was needed and to visit Eastnor for a chat. In the kitchen Ned assured us that he could lose two stone and asked us to find him a suitable horse. Ned's riding style was very old fashioned and 'jockey' never really described him.

On a mission to view a potential mount we got talking and in conversation I inquired about what he did for a living. 'I'm a venture capitalist,' he answered. Not the sort of person I meet every day, so enquired a bit more in an attempt to increase the horse purchase budget. 'What sort of businesses do you invest in then?' Ned replied, 'Have you heard of Betfair?' I nodded. 'Well, I've just sold one percent.'

He didn't mention how much he had retained. Betfair is an online betting site worth millions if not billions, so I felt assured of his ability to pay training fees. We duly found a horse and prepared it and Ned for action. The horse was easy to train; Ned not so. Just before Christmas Ned said to expect a hamper from his family farm shop. True to his word, a cool box package was delivered and I googled the source; 'Cranbourne Estates.' I was gobsmacked to discover the family own a good deal of Dorset and Ned's father was Lord Salisbury, one time Leader of the House of Lords.

However, Ned was very down to earth, took his dieting very seriously and did ride at twelve stone. On the day of the point-to-point we legged him up,

Chapter 7

led him to the start and pointed him in the right direction. On one occasion at Weston Park, he was unseated early on in a race and instead of reporting to a doctor for a post-fall medical clearance, he went straight to the beer tent, where he teamed up with Darkie Markie, the bricklayer from Malvern who was race-riding at the time. Ned's highlight as a jockey was staying on and finishing third at Brampton Bryan. He didn't ride much after that, but retained an interest in the yard for a few years.

***

I do have another connection with the corridors of power. As a teenager in the Brecon Pony Club, myself and Alistair were the only boys at camp for several summers. They were great times and my first ever proper girlfriend was a girl called Kate. She was the 'brilliantly bonkers' Kate Bingham who many years later was credited with being the person responsible for obtaining the UK's Covid-19 vaccine ahead of the rest of Europe.

CHAPTER 8

GONE WITH THE WIND AND OTHER EQUINE ISSUES

With wind showing as a most important limitation to a horse's racing performance, it's puzzling how little attention is given to it in the world of breeding. How many stallions have had sneaky wind ops that connections have conveniently forgotten about in his marketing? Rather than using stock with good wind, the routineness of wind operations means it isn't a concerning criteria and is continuing to show as a defect in offspring. Indeed, most horses that arrive at Eastnor have already been hobdayed.

I never really understood how much horses' wind affected them and their races until we owned one called Asparagus. Our main gallop through the deer park raises 300 feet over four and a half furlongs, and is a challenge to walk up as a mere human. The natural ground and steep incline often brings wind issues to the surface. Many all-weather gallops have too much spring and bounce to them, meaning the horses have an unnaturally easy time of their galloping work. On the grass here at Eastnor, you can get a true handle on horses' fitness and wind issues. They learn how to breath and gulp at certain markers up the inclines.

This can be remarkably consistent in some horses. We have learned that most horses that perform staged gulping on the gallop, and/or run with their necks outstretched, need the help of the tongue strap. This consists of a length of ladies nylon stocking which is looped tightly around horses tongue and then strapped and tied to the bottom jaw. This prevents the tongue going to the back of the mouth and obstructing the flow of air into the lungs. If a racehorse can't breathe, it struggles to race.

Asparagus was caught by his wind at a similar point on the gallops at home and in his races, and dramatically improved once we applied a tongue strap. Had Asparagus always been trained on the all-weather, his wind issue may not have been obvious.

Recent developments with overland endoscopies and improved surgery techniques have confirmed many of my suspicions, and proven on more than one occasion that horses don't have to make a noise to have a wind problem. Illustratively, we once overland-scoped a mare showing disappointment in her races. We galloped her until she ground to a halt with exhaustion. The scope revealed no defects, but we tried a tongue strap anyway. And her performance was much improved. This also tells us that it very hard to create true race conditions at home.

Sore shins are another massive cause of underperformance in racehorses. However, they are very hard to assess and identify due to being subject to so many variables (ground conditions, race trip, race speed, maturity of the horse) and the nature of horses being animals (namely, the inability to tell us what hurts). It is an extremely painful condition. Once a horse has experienced it, they are likely to never exert themselves to that point again.

They are not always a result from impact on hard ground: rather, when they are asked to extend and gallop close to or at their maximum, and the leg is stretched to its maximum length. Thus, a horse may travel well in a race until the closing stages, when the jockey is asking full effort and extension from the horse. The memory of pain prevents sore shin sufferers from responding. Sometimes they can run well when fresh, but won't exert themselves to achieve another win until they have come down the handicap enough to allow a race to be run within their comfort zone.

A young horse may run their best race first time out and never match the performance again, with form tailing off, or they may recover from it and end up stronger; thus ceasing to suffer from sore shins in the future. Tendons are well attended after a race: checking, icing and bandaging etc, but shins are often overlooked. And, as they recover quickly, it is a small window within which they can be detected. They may not cause the horse an issue again until the next critical point of exertion. Some horses will try as hard as the last time it hurt again, others won't. Sore shins affect each horse differently, at different times and will be responded to differently. Thus, they are something you will always learn more and more about. There is a case to argue that the condition dictates the class that the horse achieves, a hard-to-put-your-finger reason why horses stop improving. The other reason is the handicapper.

One of my horses, Star Angler, was a good illustration of this issue. After buying him privately, I heard from his previous trainer Henry Daly that he suffered from chronic sore shins. The horse worked well at home and was fit. Star Angler won a race at Uttoxeter, on very dry heavy ground. The horses were punching holes into the surface but coming home dry and clean. I theorised that such ground prevented the field from accelerating to the point of exertion, and from maximising stride length, which would have triggered Star Angler's sore shins. They were all forced to take pluggy, short strides. As a result: he won, quite impressively. Bizarrely, on one occasion at Bangor-on-Dee the jockey rode him to the start, notified the starter that he wasn't happy with the horse's action and the horse was withdrawn. Puzzled, looking for half an answer we came to the conclusion that the horse had stretched out and extended himself on the very wet sloppy ground, went 'Ouch, that hurts!' and on reaching the start was a hobbling wreck. Winning a race with that horse ranks as an achievement.

Another sore shin assumption was a horse I spotted running against our hurdler All Good Things. Running my eye over the form of the competition I noted Yulong Magicreef. Its first run at The Curragh in a three-year-old maiden over one mile and two furlongs on good to firm ground, he finished sixth of eighteen beaten three and a half lengths by Galileo Chrome, a future St Leger Classic winner. The fifth horse home, just in front, was Serpentine, who won the Epsom Derby two runs later. A good example of a horse trying its best on its first outing, showing fair ability but possibly returning very sore and proved reluctant to try as hard again. Which might explain why he was lowered to running in a lowly 0-100 conditional jockeys race at Ffos Las in midwinter.

Another sore shin story revolves around a horse called Idlewild. He was a point-to-pointer with so much ability on the gallops that we were very hopeful he would make up into a really good racehorse. At the racecourse he would travel and jump supremely well, looking all over the winner and just at the moment when an extra half an inch of stride was required to seal the race he would throw his head in the air, practically pull himself up and gallop up and down on the spot allowing his rival to win. He developed a reputation as being very ungenuine and was awarded a Timeform type double squiggle to label him as an arrant rogue. He finished second many times and it was only on a couple of occasions that his shins handled badly because he rarely extended his stride enough to trigger the pain.

During the Foot and Mouth epidemic of 2000/01, the authorities stopped all horse riding on the grass, to avoid cross contamination with cloven footed beasts. So we were prevented from using our gallops. Although there was some farm subsidy type set-aside land which hadn't had livestock on it in living memory they didn't have a fence to enclose livestock and we had nowhere to exercise except on the road. DEFRA wouldn't allow the estate to have a double income from the land in use or non-use (as in a payment for not farming the land and a payment/income for use as a gallop).

Chapter 8

A local businessman and racehorse owner kindly agreed to hire us his private all-weather gallop on a pro-rata basis. It was a good half hour of road work to get there but we had little option as it was closest and boxing multiple lots was not going to work without hiring expensive transport. The gallop in question was wood fibre and has the steepest incline of any artificial gallop I have ever used. All our horses had been accustomed to a natural grass type of training and found the gallop and the surface alien with the necessary stride reach needed to attain the summit a hard task. But our horses were fit and I was slightly bemused as to why they found it such hard work.

When we had finished the morning's work and were feeding round at lunch time several of the young horses were scraping with their front legs and showing signs of being shin sore and a usual handle and examination confirmed this. You could argue that the unusual long distant hike on the hard-metalled road was too much and as far as I could tell it was a bizarre short-term discomfort. But trainers on that site prior to our use of the facility and subsequent trainers based at the yard managed to produce very few winners. Makes you think! Sore shins will always teach you something, if you can spot them.

A dressage eventing type had acquired a relatively young thoroughbred originally to retrain but fancied that she would like to run the gelding back under Rules even though its racing form was very average. We did a deal which including her riding and exercising the horse as many days of the week as she could. The horse was fairly fit but carrying too much condition. It was working well and we were beginning to get a little excited that it wouldn't let us down when we ran.

The owner then revealed that the previous connections had given up on a racing career because of sore shins. I informed her of my views and experience of these matters, but she was convinced that her dressage-type flat work had changed the horse's action and that sore shins wouldn't be a problem.

At the racecourse it was the same old story, travel and jump nicely until push came to shove and an extra inch of stride was required; the horse said, 'I don't think so.' The next day examination of the shins proved to be painless and it took some explaining to the owner my theory, but the horse had remembered his previous exertions when he willingly tried his best and made himself hurt like hell and declined to go there again. We ran him a couple more times with the same result before calling it a day.

There is a story about a jockey dismounting from a disappointing run and declaring to the glum owners that their pride and joy had made a noise. They enquired as to whether it was a gurgle or a whistle and were unamused to hear it described as an 'Eeyore!'

CHAPTER 9

STAYING ON THE CAROUSEL: SURVIVING THE BUSINESS OF TRAINING

One of the most difficult tasks facing a trainer is keeping up momentum. There is a theory that all you need is one good horse to set you up for a stellar career of riches and fame. In truth, you need a supply of good horses being nurtured in a consistent stream. It works two ways.
1. Throwing a lot of money at some expensive well bred horses, many of which will prove to be moderate or unsound.
2. Throwing a lot of money at loads of moderately bred cheap horses and hoping a star emerges. Obviously this way you spend a great deal of your funds finding out through your training bills. It amuses me when a cheaply bought two-year-old wins a good prize up north and the racing press herald the story of how, in reality, the trainer picked up this nugget for a bargain basement minimum bid of £600 at the yearling sales, has zero breeding and moves like a box of spanners...and yet it is 'Well bought' and 'well trained.' Connections have been bid big dollars from overseas. They neglect to mention that at that particular auction, the trainer in question bought twenty for the minimum bid and the rest are useless, rehomed or dead!

The problem with training lots of moderate, cheap horses to win races is that you tend to get sent more moderate, cheap horses, and once they have peaked, they need to be moved on to start with a fresh team. The worst thing a trainer can do is persevere with proven or over-exposed rubbish. You need to have fresh blood coming through the ranks all the time. If you are lucky enough to have more than one good horse at any one time, milk that moment for as long as you can, because it won't last.

Loads of trainers have five minutes of fame. A big Saturday winner. The media build you up, hail you as a miracle worker. You sit at home waiting for the phone to ring, Owners falling over themselves to send you horses, but nothing happens. You go through a quiet spell as all yards do and the media suggest that you have lost it or suddenly can't train. Over the years I have seen some really good trainers fall off the edge, for various reasons: personal, financial, mental... Some of them throw away an awful lot of personal wealth to live their dream. I live my dream, but in a realistic sort of way!

Trainers have to put up with an awful lot of criticism. If you make the wrong call about where to run, for example. The pundits question your motives or reasons for a certain entry, when if they knew that there were zero options for a particular horse in the programme book they may understand the logic. You have to be very careful what information you release as it can often get you into more trouble telling the truth than if you had said nothing. Many times I may run a horse locally just to give the owners a day out in a race that isn't perfect because the options were few, and you may as well travel 30 miles to run badly and have a nice day out as travel 100 miles for the same result. Hopefully the majority of owners can see that I am trying my best to generate maximum experience and fun for them, and although I try to limit unnecessary expense, I hope they deem my efforts as satisfactory!

Nine times out of ten when an owner moves on for whatever reason it is a relief. If the said owner is not happy with level of my service and hard work trying to train his moderate horse to perform to the best of its ability, then tough. As usual it's one or more less payers, and the timing can often be when finances are tight but the majority of times it works out for the best. Numerous times something turns up that is unexpected to raise spirits and faith in the human race and keep me in business.

I often consider how I managed to get this far in the racing game? Sir Mark Prescott has defined success in training as simply staying on the carousel, year after year. Now it's harder than ever. How have I survived?

I've been very lucky in life. I was raised in the countryside on a farm with a strong family and instilled work ethic: to be frugal and not live beyond my means. I have never been a lucky gambler but I generally never bet above my limit. Having said that, my discipline in that department has been wayward, but in the sense of losing £100 (a very rare large wager for me) on a horse that lost, rather than thousands.

I don't consider myself to be lucky in business. Yes, I have managed to stay in business and attract owners to keep afloat. But any bloodstock speculation generally results in a loss. Thankfully my low level investment loss can be absorbed. For example, a £5,000 bloodstock disaster can be absorbed. A £50,000 disaster not so!

I am very lucky to be married to a low maintenance wife, except for her hunters, whose expense can be absorbed into the business.

Chapter 9

On a filthy wet winter's day at Ludlow, back in the early days, I was in conversation with John Mackie, a trainer who I have a great deal of time for. He has a wry outlook on the world with a down-to-earth wise answer for every situation and questions about life, the universe and everything. The rain was horizontal and our heads were bent, faces down and he mentioned my very inappropriate shoes for the weather conditions. They were bog-standard cheap Marks and Spencer's deck shoes that I had already owned for at least three years. They had absorbed plenty of moisture and my feet were soggy. It dawned on me that these were the only shoes I had, let alone a best pair, a work pair or any other kind of pair. A frugal life but necessary to keep afloat.

You have to start out with a business plan, find a niche, know what is possible to achieve and be realistic. Dreaming of training lots of nice young horses to win novice hurdles is fantasy for someone like me. So many novice hurdle winners progress to win very little more, due to being allotted an unrealistic handicap mark and becoming disappointing. The sport punishes you and your runners for trying their best and exposing their probably limited ability for all to see. If the rewards, i.e. prizemoney were to be more generous then it would pay for every horse to run on its merits, to achieve its best placing for prizemoney because the money won would be worth it. UK racing is the best in the world for quality but is a laughing stock for levels of prize money

I am happy-go-lucky. I have many a disappointing day or result and I can get up the next morning and start all over again. You must never let a bad day get you down. Some people watch the race replays of a poor run over and over again, looking for a jockey error or a random reason for why their horse failed expectations, which were probably unrealistic in the first place! They rarely accept 'because it wasn't fucking good enough' as a reason!

Yes, it is a vocation! Yes, it is tougher at the bottom. But there are rewards. They are meagre at my level, in return for the time, effort and heartache, but it is very satisfying to train a moderate animal to win a race for some nice owners and make them smile. In a bigger picture, every time I have a runner, my name is in every single newspaper with racing coverage. I have only once been interviewed after a terrestrial TV win, but speak reasonably often on the specialist racing channels. I have a fair share of fancied runners who gamblers are prepared to follow because of my reputation as a trainer whose horses are fit, well prepared and always trying to run to the best of their ability with no jiggery-pokery.

Seek The Faith (l) and Now We Know (r) both 5th at Cheltenham Festival in my first year training, 1996.

Deliceo (Jim Culloty)

There are some trainers who never have a fancied runner or a favourite. There are some trainers whose winners are so rare it is an embarrassment. They may have all the facilities, all the bullshit, but zero clue. There are trainers with dubious owners, trainers proven to have dodgy connections. Trainers given second chances after serious breaches of the rules. Applying for licences after a time away, by which time all the staff on the licensing team have moved on and nobody can remember what a lying fuckwit they were the first time around. It beggars belief that on disqualification of a trainer (who becomes a warned-off person) that a licence is happily issued to the spouse and that the individual is expected to have no involvement in the business.

At the end of the day horseracing is just horses galloping round a field, and some go faster than others. Gambling adds a lot of interest and for some people it adds a lot of liability. In training horses, you can only do your best with the ammunition available. It doesn't matter how you train a horse, if the animal is of limited ability it won't win any race above its class. Form is temporary, and class or lack of it - is permanent! What not everyone seems to understand is that when a horse has hit form and maybe run up a sequence of wins or good placed runs it is raised up in the weights by the handicapper and the trainer is forced to up the horse in class. If the horse has stopped improving then the extra weight and stronger competition will give the impression that maybe the horse has run badly, when in reality it just wasn't good enough on that day.

You can have the best breeding, perfect conformation, best paces, be trained by the most proven trainer and could still be devoid of ability. You can tweak wind or allow horse to mature. Change its routine, change its races. You can spend a lot of money doing everything perfectly correct for every single horse and still only some will be any good and make the grade. No matter how much they cost. They are animals.

There was a time when a cheaply purchased horse could have a chance of winning its cost back in prize money, but those days are gone and winning a realistic prize with an expensive horse to cover its purchase price is cloud cuckoo land.

Then you can have a local home bred with no breeding, poor conformation, no relations of note: a complete freak in all departments and it could be a class animal.

Chapter 9

Norton's Coin is a good example of small player hitting the big time and winning the Cheltenham Gold Cup. Trained and owned by a dairy farmer from West Wales who only trained his own horses he beat all the big names as a 100/1 outsider. Fairy tale stuff. I was at a Welsh point-to-point back in the 1980s and top amateur rider Tim Jones had just won on the horse in very impressive fashion. In conversation, he said to me, 'That horse will win a Gold Cup one day.'

Yeah-yeah! Raised eyebrows! But the horse did win that pinnacle of National Hunt horse racing. Legend has it that when Tim went to the Tote window to collect some of his many winnings, they supplied some carrier bags for him to carry it all.

I have never lived beyond my means. I have rarely borrowed money from the bank and never buy anything unless I can afford it. You have to make things last. Your daily riding-out tack, your horses, your staff, and in this game, it is a really good idea to make your wife last, by putting her first.

***

Heard over the tannoy at a point-to-point after the Ladies race when there were plenty of empty saddles. 'Will all the fallen women please report to the doctor?'

CHAPTER 10

TRAINING OWNERS

There is no doubt that more winners can be achieved when owner interference is minimal. However, as previously suggested, economics and owner necessity or demands steer you down a path of being bullied into unrealistic scenarios. Sometimes you have to try and manipulate an owner to agree to a certain plan and try and make them think it was their own idea. When discussing racing plans my favourite leading phrase is, 'What I would like to do is, if that's OK with you, is….'

In my efforts to be a trainer, my policy of being honest and trying my best has backfired on me on more than one occasion. Doing deals is always going to end messily. Some owners have short memories. You could do a special deal or a mate's rate for them, but later they are the slowest to pay or jump ship after some disappointing runs. They can also be extremely fickle.

I remember an occasion when I was incredibly honest with an owner. He had a lovely little grey horse and it was sent to us having been broken in as a three-year-old. It was very, very weak, but its work was quite good at home so we sent it down to Exeter for a bumper (a National Hunt Flat race). It got beaten quite a long way. The owner called round after the race, with plans for another bumper up in Newcastle in about three weeks' time. To be fair, there were very few other options. Actually, none. I said I was doing him a favour by not trucking all the way up to the north east, with all the accompanying costs, to have the same performance as that at Exeter; that his horse needed six months to strengthen up and then it would be better placed to continue its career.

As usual, the owner took offence, disappeared and sent the horse to another trainer. It reappeared six months later and had a few quite good runs but nothing of note, and then they put it in a claiming hurdle at Chepstow. I think it finished third or fourth. Another trainer spotted its potential and claimed it, and eventually it got up to a rating of 135 and won a load of races. It was always a disappointment to me that if the owner had stuck with me or sent it back to me, we could have had some serious fun and some great days racing.

If an owner sets me a realistic target race, I will do everything in my power to achieve that goal. I am a great believer in running horses when times are right, as there are so many times when they aren't. Be it the wrong ground, a lack of suitable races, owners' availability or minor equine injuries. Owners are paying me for a service: for them to be able to watch their horses perform. I do have a reputation for running my horses too often; but as with most aspects in life there two sides to every story. Some owners like it, as they feel that they are getting value for money. And still get snotty when something prevents their horse from making a target race. But I will admit that some owners have reined me in when I got carried away.

Another time I bought a new horse out of Ireland for an owner. It was very good value and turned out to be an absolute pony of a thing. The owner was one of these gentlemen who insisted on riding it himself as much as possible. Just before it was due to run he gave me a list of five of the top ten jockeys that he wanted to ride it in races. All very good riders but the chances of any of them being available to be the mare's regular partner were remote, to say the least. When I questioned his thinking and pointed out if he was to be part of Team Eastnor he could expect to have my son Stan ride the horse, he replied, 'I like the way you train and I like that I can come and ride it out, but I don't want your boy riding it in races. A matter of choice.'

So I suggested he might choose another trainer, at which point he backed down and Stan proceeded to win two races on the horse. The same owner had previously had a horse in training and insisted on riding it himself daily. Being a heavy full-grown man, he overworked the horse until it fell out of love with the game. We did win a very bad race before he sold it cheaply to a point-to-point yard who sweetened the horse up and trained him to win some high class hunter chases, just by not being so hard on the horse. Did I mention owner interference elsewhere cost us winners?

If an owner wants to have a horse in training with you they will. It doesn't matter how good your facilities are, what your location is, how much you charge, your website, or your statistics. Most owners like to jump on to 'Flavour of the Day' trainer bandwagons, or young claiming jockey bandwagons. Just as the bloodstock world like to jump on stallion bandwagons. Some bandwagons can keep on rolling but quite often the wheels fall off!

Over the years there have been periods of a small Matt Sheppard bandwagon. We may have had an exceptional season at our local tracks with some cheaply sourced, well handicapped, low-grade and sound horses which win and run consistently well for connections, and therefore become popular and talked about.

The following season we still have the same horses, but now they are in the grip of the handicapper, and are no longer performing. They still cost the same to keep, even though we have been honest and hinted to owners that they are unlikely to improve or win any time soon. New owners have hopped on the bandwagon and sent more cheap horses which they have invariably bought or bred themselves, and most of which are unlikely to be winners. Thus follows a very poor year. We haven't changed, or done anything differently, but still we go from hero to zero.

This tends to be cyclical. Good year, poor year, regroup, good year. Bandwagon owners leave, we regroup, move duff horses on. At our level it is very hard to attract high-net-worth owners and improve the quality of our string. Instead, we need to have new horses coming through in the system all the time to keep up vital momentum, as mentioned before.

When I first started training I judged that for every four owners that supported the yard, one might develop into a long term owner. Now it is lucky if one in ten stay and that is maybe ten new owners in ten years. I do, however, have zero bad debts, and only once have had to resort to legal action to ensure payment.

Nowadays owners drift in, looking for deals, gambles and excitement. They may come on the recommendation of a friend who is into looking at trainer statistics. It is noticeable to me that the big West Country owners tend to share their horses about with all the local trainers. Here in the West Midlands it seems to be completely the opposite. They have their horses trained miles away. I don't know why.

You can guarantee that when an owner jumps ship to a different trainer or yard on some quest for a better gallop, different jockey, cheaper daily rate (probably with more extras) that they indirectly encourage the owners you have left to join them for the greener grass.

As much as I am lucky to have owners who love racing and love horses, they sometimes have no conception of any of the daily risks we expose ourselves to. When we suggest that a horse is not a particular nice conveyance, i.e. tries to kill us most days, they chuckle and say "Bless him". Or, if we let them know that the vet will invoice them for some sedative to allow us to clip safely, they have no idea how dangerous a situation we put ourselves in during the process of finding that out. We have even had owners' wives comment on some shaky clipping lines on a hind leg to which the reply is, 'You are welcome to clip your horse yourself, Madam.'

Chapter 10

But swallowing the oversights and embracing the lack of knowledge is all part of the job.

A classic example of success not helping you to succeed is Shaun Lycett's epic triumph to be leading summer jumps trainer at Worcester one year, beating all the leading trainers with big strings. Training some moderate horses very well to run consistently, win and stay sound on summer ground was a huge achievement for a small yard. Did it propel him to superstardom? No. Did he get sent so many new horses he had to get more staff? No. Did he get sent a load of moderate horses with zero ability? Probably!

I once had a really difficult owner who lived locally, and considered himself a saviour or benefactor of small trainers in Herefordshire. He mainly owned moderate home-breds, including a particularly reckless hurdler called Winter Rose. He should have won a race, but the owners were insistent about running locally at Worcester in a level weights novice hurdle instead of a handicap off a favourable mark. And, as usual in these scenarios, the horse finished second and the handicapper upped his mark by twelve pounds, even though it did not win. Not for the first nor last time, owner interference cost a winner to my tally.

The horse did win for his next trainer but took a whole year of racing to get his mark reduced to a winnable one.

Full of good intentions, but generally unrealistic about the whole sport, we had a trip to the Tattersalls Derby Sale in search of a young horse to follow on from Winter Rose. We purchased a value for money 'unbroken' but well-handled four-year-old by Phardante. I am always a tad suspicious when a young horse lunges and long reins like a pro, especially when getting on them proves to be a challenge. This lad proved no exception. At one point we would leave him tacked up and one of us would be legged up in the stable every fifteen minutes all day. One problem was the fact that they had been worked hard pre-sale to make sure they passed the vet cert wind examination. As a result, they are fairly fit and therefore difficult to get tired enough to move on to next stage of breaking. This horse was a disappointment on the track and 'needed more time.' It ran out in a bumper and generally didn't want to know. The owner talked of buying another and I was keen not go down the same young-horse route, but at the time I had one for sale belonging to David Redvers. It was a reasonably bred mare but very backward, and because of this I made no effort to sell her to this owner. Next thing I knew he had approached

David Redvers off his own bat, bought the mare and sent it to Venetia Williams. It lasted there about two months and never ran in its life but did breed some winners. Later the owner wrote a book about his racing life and included that the reason I didn't punt him the said mare was because I wanted it for myself, when in fact all I was trying to do was save him some more disappointment and money by not having another backward horse in training. He seemed to forget in his memoir that I was right about the mare's prospects, but as ever my good intentions for my clients were overlooked.

Why are owners and breeders obsessed with insisting that all race horses will be better over a further distance? One of the main observations I noted working for Arthur Moore is to always campaign the young horses over the minimum trip until you are happy that they are strong enough to cope with an increase in trip. Sometimes you have to form your own view. Jockeys can mislead you. They don't know what to say after a poor run and say a longer trip might suit. I have been wrong many times but on occasions a drop in trip has been an inspired call.

The older I get the more my eyes are opened to what is really going on and the more I realise that there is nothing I can do about it. There is no doubt that if you are a small trainer with small time owners it is very hard to attract high rollers. Big owners like to mix with other big owners and compete and brag about which of them have the biggest cheque book and they don't seem to care that the bloodstock agents are swimming like sharks ready to extract a huge sum and calculating their percentage – probably from both sides. If you plough your own furrow, purchase value for money racehorses on your judgement and avoid the cesspool of corruption of dodgy deals you will definitely not be in the clique. In the days of the old Doncaster Bloodstock Sales I was in the bar after the last lot had been sold and in banter with a well-known agent. He described how 'we have been trying to get so and so (a rich Yank) to buy a horse on his own instead of having shares in big exclusive type syndicates and we got him here to the sales and bang, we nailed him.' I said, 'You're a bloodstock agent, you are not supposed to nail anyone.' End of conversation. If you are in the clique and use the agents they probably manage and advise owners and will recommend you as trainer. If you don't use them, good luck!

Chapter 10

Lost in the Summer Wine

The Lost in the Summer Wine National Hunt syndicate was formed from members of a successful point-to-point syndicate called the Bean Club which was run by Nicky's sister Susie. The first horse to run under Rules in the syndicate name was Lost In The Snow (Arctic Lord ex Where Am I). He was a cheap purchase who was sound and gave us a lot of fun. He won a fast ground maiden point at Chaddesley Corbett before being aimed at summer jumping in the 2005 season. Once he had run three times to achieve a lowly handicap mark he was placed quite a few times over hurdles and fences on fast ground including when second under Paddy Brennan, who declared that Snowy was the worst horse he had ever ridden!

The next horse was Fair Shake, a very sweet horse with loads of mileage on the clock who was placed several times and won a race on heavy ground on a filthy day at Stratford in August 2008. It was a 0-100 handicap hurdle worth a handsome (then) £4,000 to the winner! It was the last race, the winners enclosure was under water and only the winning connections were there to celebrate. During the soggy prize giving I heard some funny thwacking sort of sounds and turned round to see many drunken racegoers falling out of the bar fighting and kicking. The sound was of fists and punches connecting with flesh. Fair Shake was also unlucky not to win another race when looking to have a good chance but for falling at second last at Exeter. He was retired to a good home with one of the members and is still going in 2024.

Next up was Pin D'Estruval, a cheap horse from Arthur Moore that had ability but more than a few issues. When we first started riding him he was very awkward and took a lot of sitting as he would whip round to the left doing doughnut-like circles. As he was in the last chance saloon we tried various tricks to solve the problem. In the end we tried a straight rubber bar bit and he never whipped round again and became a very good ride. On his first run at Stratford on the Monday of Cheltenham week he was in a very commanding position leading three fences out when turning a somersault. Jockey David Dennis came back carrying his left elbow in his right hand and his thumb was practically touching his bicep. It proved to be a career ending injury. The horse did win a race over fences for Charlie Poste, who then became my first choice jockey.

These first three horses cost a total of £4,500. The next horse, Witness That, cost a bit more and proved a disappointment with various problems before Faustina Pius was purchased at Doncaster Sales in November 2013 for £5,500. She won two chases at Stratford ridden by Stan and was retired to stud after sustaining a tendon injury. Percy's Choice was next. He was placed before going down with grass sickness. Then came Orion's Might, who became a frustrating individual. He was bought privately from Ireland and arrived with an unrealistic hurdle rating and his early runs for us were good enough for it not to be lowered significantly. After several placed efforts Stan gave him a blinding ride to make all and win at Uttoxeter where he headlined for winning his first race at his 51st attempt. He was a cranky ride at home and his eyesight was later found to be defective.

Freebie

Mazovian was a Darley American-bred gelding that originally went through the sales for £800. He was bought by a trainer called Michael Chapman, for whom he ran over 60 times on the flat. Michael Chapman was not a particularly significant trainer. Mazovian was claimed for £6,000 after finishing fourth in a selling hurdle at Stratford, and went to join top trainer Neil Mulholland. He went on to win one race with him on the all-weather at Southwell. The punters who claimed him in the seller had probably not looked at Mazovian in the flesh at all. They just looked at his breeding and his form and bought him off that, seeing that it could be improved. He was obviously sound as it had run 60 times! He was offered to me as a free horse by some gambling connections. I thought I'd give him a chance, and offered him to the Lost in the Summer Wine syndicate as 'fit and ready to run.' I collected him from Strensham services, briefly examining him as we swapped lorries. His near fore fetlock was enormous, but the girl who was with him said that was normal, and explained why he was £800. He had come to me as a freebie as it would not have been cost effective to send him through the sales. He proved to be an excellent ride and Eastnored well, while saving plenty for himself. We managed to win a £4,000 race at Ludlow before deciding he'd had enough of racing. He had, after all, ran 82 times.

Cry Fury followed and was placed a couple of times over fences, then a grey mare called Rule The Ocean who took a little time to find her feet before some places over hurdles and fences. Rathbride Prince was a complete disaster with little ability or will. Star of Oscar suffered an aneurysm before making it to the track. Getawaytonewbay was a summer horse while Getafriend's 'work in progress' status came to an end when he dogged it at Warwick in a novice hurdle. He had already put me in hospital for five days and although there was some ability he needed to try harder. In our daily routine we subject ourselves to measured daily risks. We have ridden hundreds of different horses in our lives and we know when to call it a day. I sent a WhatsApp video call to Paul Smith, who runs the syndicate, after his poor run and he forwarded it on to his club members. My message was pragmatic and strong. The horse was the most dangerous that we had anything to do with and his temper was off the scale. I gave them the recommendation that there was no chance of finding a home for him and that a bullet was the only option. Four members phoned me. Three to support my decision and one to ask if there was any medication available i.e., Valium or Prozac.

The group had some luck when Getawaytonewbay sluiced up at Stratford in April 2021.

The syndicate is very well run by Paul. Members come and go but the original hardcore base has been solid from the start and Paul's management and integrity is second to none. With a small budget they have enjoyed and experienced every high and low in the game and I am very lucky to have their support.

Spin off horses from this team included San Marco, who won three hurdle races and was placed over fences for the JMK syndicate headed by long-time supporter Robert Kujawa, and Brave Villa.

Brave Villa

Purchased from Arthur Moore at Doncaster sales for £5,000, Brave Villa had some average form in Ireland but was just the type of horse to be Eastnored. On his first run for us at Worcester he finished second and came up the run in with his neck stretched out. The jockey Dave Dennis suggested blinkers but my hunch was that his high head carriage suggested difficulty breathing, and a tongue strap would help. Duly applied, he finished second at Bangor-on-Dee to a well handicapped French horse of Alan King's which was running off a mark of 102 and subsequently achieved 140 plus. He was a very consistent horse who loved soft ground and always ran well fresh. I recall winning the feature race of the day at Taunton just before the Cheltenham Festival and receiving zero mention in the *Racing Post*, which really cheesed me off. He was also one of only two runners in my career that I consider was stopped by a jockey. I suppose two out of two thousand runners is probably not a bad statistic. There are plenty of runners that get 'no ride', but a runner given no ride in order to let another horse win is a fairly serious offence. However, the plan backfired as the horse that was supposed to win got nutted on the line.

Towards the end of his racing career, Brave Villa had a very hard race at Newbury and didn't want to know after that. The handicapper had forced him up and up in grade and he was from a family of rogues. But he was a slow two miler and won us five chases and £35,000 starting with a rating of 83 and achieving 119 at his peak.

***

Talking to a potential owner at the races and discussing a recent rumour that one high profile owner had disposable income of £4m a month. The gentleman said, 'Yeah, I have 10% of that,' but he never sent me a horse to train.

CHAPTER 11

HORSES FOR COURSES:
A 'WHO'S WHO' OF EASTNOR'S HALL OF FAME

Here are some horses that have been trained at Eastnor, not mentioned in the previous or later chapters, who achieved various levels of success and have some interesting tales around their time at Home Farm.

Seek The Faith (my first winner)
After a couple of seasons of point-to-pointing, we decided to bite the bullet and take out a professional licence. Following that, Julian Pritchard's father Edward introduced me to a farmer from the Forest of Dean called Frank Matthews.

I had some inside information about Seek The Faith from Dermot Weld's: he was an incredible workhorse with plenty of ability, but I got the impression that he had been used as a yardstick to help the trainer prep his young horses, and as a result was completely washed out mentally.

It was the first horse for which I went to the sales with no idea of the budget in hand. We went to the Doncaster October Sale and Mrs Mercy Rimell, for whom I worked when I first got into racing, was sitting behind Mr Matthews and myself in the bidding arena. When the bidding reached £12,000, which was a lot of money back in 1995, she gave him a nudge, 'Bid again!' So we did, and got the horse for £13,000; the only time that I ever will top an auction and Jonjo O'Neill be the under-bidder.

As usual, Frank had someone with him who was a complete foreigner to horse racing and yet thought he knew everything, who couldn't believe he had spent that money on a horse when plenty were going through for £500. Owners' friends...

Before his first run at Chepstow, Brendan Powell senior had come to school the horse over our jumps. Alarmingly, he turned a complete somersault over one of our baby fences. So, in the time before the race Julian Pritchard, top amateur rider and horseman, spent many hours with Seek The Faith (SID) and got him jumping really well.

In the race at Chepstow, Brendan gave the horse no ride at all until after the last, when he sprinted up the run in to win by a neck at 50/1, beating a really good horse called Challenger Du Luc. This was my first winner as a licensed trainer.

I remember the first time I sat on Seek The Faith. I immediately thought he was an absolutely class individual. He loved being at Eastnor, he loved being on the grass, he loved being in the deer park and he loved being turned out, none of which would have happened where he came from in Ireland. The horse was wasted because the owner was very unrealistic. We had to go to Chepstow and Cheltenham and were exposed to far too many uninformed opinions. The owner used to go regularly to Gloucester Market on a Monday and all of his farming friends would wind him up, filling him with all manner of crazy ideas and suggestions of how to campaign the horse. On the Monday night Mr Matthews would ring me up and relay all the new plans.

He finished fifth in an Arkle at Cheltenham, a two mile novice chase at the Festival and a great achievement for my first runner. Frank then insisted on running in two Champion Chases, because 'he wanted to meet the Queen Mother.' I did point out that in order to do this, you had to do more than just take part in the race: indeed, you needed to win it, and the poor horse was completely outclassed off level weights taking on One Man et al. He did have an entry one year in the two mile Grand Annual Handicap Chase and would have had an excellent chance of being a Festival winner, but Mr Matthews wouldn't budge.

We had a great day at Newbury in February 1998 when Richard Johnson won on him and provide half of my first double. Another horse I trained called Now We Know won over 3m5f at Bangor.

Richard Dunwoody gave Seek The Faith a brilliant ride to win at Cheltenham on some very firm ground which was not his preference. With all the miles on his clock he took a long time to recover.

At the end of the day I was given a brief by a difficult owner to fulfil a dream of winning a race at his local track and at the cathedral of horse racing, Cheltenham, which I achieved – but with less owner interference it could have been so much more. He won at Chepstow, Cheltenham and Newbury but every race I wanted to target became an argument, 'Chepstow or Cheltenham?' A ten-win career at Eastnor with this horse was definitely within the realms of possibility.

In the end, Seek The Faith's wind deteriorated and the owner sent him to another trainer where he didn't do very well. He enjoyed a long and happy retirement with the Greatwood rehabilitation charity.

Oatis Rose

This mare was sent by David Redvers of Tweenhills Stud in his pre-flat racing days. She was a tiny, slight mare. In the days when I had a horse weighing scales her racing weight was around 440kgs. At some point her owners had tried to make a show horse out of her and had trimmed her feet to fit her dainty body. Our old fashioned farrier at the time let her feet grow to her natural size which turned out to look enormous at the end of her spindly legs. Previous to this change she had a very choppy stride but as she grew more foot her action and stride length improved because her feet were no longer sore. No foot, no horse, as the saying goes.

Oatis Rose had some good relatives. After a bumper run she did have some fair runs in novice hurdles and then was sent handicapping over two miles. We began to question her resolve. She then ran over two miles three furlongs at Taunton. AP McCoy rode her and reported that she needed further and a galloping track, not a sharp one like Taunton. She had qualified for the mares-only novices hurdle handicap final at Newbury in March, so an entry was made and at declaration she managed to sneak in at the bottom of the weights. There was no racing administration internet in those days (1995), so chasing a last minute jockey was a nightmare. Any previous riders weren't available. It was the early days of jockey agents but when a northern-based jockey called Paul Carberry was touted I jumped at his availability; a young rider at the time, but as good as any jockey ever and a future Irish champion. I called David's mother, who was the co-owner, and excitedly relayed the booking and she said, 'Paul who?'

In the paddock I instructed the rider to give her some space, but Paul wasn't listening. She had been brought down at the stable bend at Chepstow and broke Richard Johnson's collarbone. She disliked being crowded, but luckily on this occasion the ground was very soft and most of the field ran wide so her route down the inner was clear.

The race was on BBC1 on a Saturday afternoon and the commentator was the legendary Peter O'Sullevan. My second ever professional winner as a licensed trainer had the great man calling 'Oatis Rose, trained by Matthew Sheppard, ridden by Paul Carberry and owned by Alexander Figg.' Just hearing my name called by the great man still makes me shiver.

She was badly handicapped the following year but Adrian Maguire gave her an inspired ride to win at Sandown to beat his championship rival Richard Dunwoody by a nose. Maguire was injured shortly afterwards and her next two runs were good, but the jockey tried to go down the inner at Newbury. She should have won, but she was not brave enough to battle through horses in front. I didn't give the same jockey any instructions the next time out at Worcester and he rode her exactly the same way: down the inner with exactly the same result, hampered on the bend turning for home, took a pull to come wide around, finished fast and late but too late, and she was only placed again. She was retired to stud shortly afterwards but failed to have any offspring of note.

Burning Truth

Burning Truth (quickly known as BT on the yard - I always did love an acronym) was one of my all-time favourite horses. He was a slight, angular chestnut, incredibly narrow and the picture of a fast-ground horse; the sort of fast ground racehorse welfare doesn't allow any more. I picked him up from Doncaster Sales in August of 2003 for a bargain 2,200 guineas. He went so cheaply as a result of one of my favourite series of events.

I had picked out the horse from the information available in those days from a form book. Such study was essential homework and you could sometimes spot something that might get missed on the day. This was before punters had instant, remote access to the amount of information there is today in online catalogues. He was bought purely on form: not confirmation, not pedigree, and I didn't care what he looked like. He had run three times over hurdles and multiple times on the flat for Anne Duffield. One particular run stood out to me where he had been beaten 36 lengths by a good horse of Martin Pipe's, Puntal.

As Lot 46, Burning Truth was one of the earlier sales of the day, and he was located in a particularly dark stable. On viewing him there, I discovered his near fore below the knee was filled and sore. 'Bugger! He's broken,' I thought. Nonetheless, I asked for him to be trotted up, and he was sound. I also noticed during the trot-up a recent, weeping kick wound above his knee. His girl groom hadn't noticed. Temporary injury-related filling was no problem in my eyes. So I returned to my usual spot, twenty yards away, and watched for the rest of the morning as countless owners and trainers dismissed Burning Truth as I had almost done, quickly re-emerging from his stable with shaking heads and no further examination which meant very few were willing to risk a bid. Anne Duffield was late to the sale and found me later to say, 'You have a bargain at that price.' I don't think she knew about his wound!

Chapter 11

His first run for me was at Worcester, in September 2002. Burning Truth's owner, Mr Gordon Jones, attended along with, as is the norm it seems, his Friend Who Knew Everything. BT finished fifth in a field of 24 in a selling handicap hurdle, beaten 11 lengths, which for 2,200 guineas was a great result in my mind. Naturally the Friend was furious he didn't win as he had forecast, despite the ground being on the soft side of good which we came to learn was not how BT liked it. The more like a road the racetrack was, the better he ran.

At Hereford next time out Mr Jones's Friend Who Knew Everything failed to turn up. On the way to the start one of the reins broke and young Robert Biddlecombe did well to anchor him before he exerted himself too much. A much fitter, younger version of myself sprinted to the stables, obtained a spare set from fledgling trainer Alan King in the stable yard, fixed the bridle and we were allowed to run. With the perfect firm ground suiting BT perfectly, they jumped off, made all and were never headed. A winner at 25/1. That autumn he was an unlucky second at Wincanton before winning a nice prize at Ludlow.

The following year in April (2003), the preparation for his summer campaign began. In the week up to his run at Stratford, Alex Bevan, who rode BT out every day, was on holiday. I rode him for the seven days instead. Never have I experienced a more jarred-up horse. He felt as if he had four square wheels! He seemed very happy and forward-going enough, but his action didn't give me much confidence.

Once at Stratford, several faces asked me about BT's chances. I said I didn't really fancy him. This was before the betting exchanges – but he soon drifted to a big price. Robert Biddlecombe was riding him that day. He jumped off in front, made all, and absolutely bolted up. The faces who had been asking prior to the race returned and suggested I'd stitched them up, but I was gobsmacked. And immensely proud of the horse.

On Alex's return from holiday I quizzed her about his action. She said he had felt that way since the first time she rode him. Perhaps with her considerable experience in flat yards she was used to horses feeling jarred up and scratchy and just accepted it from day one.

In total, BT ran 28 times for Eastnor, and 20 times was in the first four. He won us five hurdle races and one chase: winnings amounting to £37,000 (and that was twenty years ago). He had an initial handicap mark of 86 and his highest winning mark was 113. Towards the end of his career, he had a couple of disappointing runs. Before what was to be his final run at Stratford,

I schooled him over hurdles as a lead horse to get a feel for him. As soon as he entered the schooling field and saw the hurdles, he took off flat out, winging everything. He must be back to form, I thought. I entered him at Stratford and he made the running as usual, trying his best as always, but he broke down after the third last hurdle. I did shed some tears.

Shortly after, I attended Gordon Jones' memorial service. In the Eulogy was the following passage: 'Gordon owned a racehorse horse called Burning Truth, who was just like Gordon. You never had to ask him; he always tried his best.' He was the ultimate Slow Two Miler. BT had such a good nature that we retired him to Newbridge Farm Park as a horse for city folk to pat and feed carrots. Still going strong in 2024!

Munlochy Bay

Munlochy Bay was owned by the Blues Partnership, headed by Simon Gegg. She won three races from 28 runs, winning a total of £20,000 in prize money. She was bought for 9,500 guineas from Doncaster Sales in August 2009, a compact bay mare with a large dent below her right eye that was apparently due to an accident as a young horse. She made a roaring noise when galloping. She won a two mile flat race at Goodwood for her previous trainer, and she showed little pieces of form over hurdles for us, before quite a remarkable run at Cheltenham in 2010. Running off a mark of 96, she was possibly the lowest rated horse ever to win a race at that track. Amateur Liam Pater, who worked for me at the time, took the ride and did nine stone eleven in order to do so. The race was a three mile handicap hurdle, run at a furious pace. Liam pushed and shoved for the duration, with the mare never once picking up the bridle. They made some progress at approaching two out, hit the front in the last hundred yards and won going away. Liam received no credit for an exceptional ride. If he'd been AP or Richard Johnson the journalists would have been all over it! Nonetheless, it was a very special day for the horse to win at Cheltenham.

She won a further two races for Charlie Poste in 2012, but was always a very hard ride, appearing as not very genuine at all and never taking the bridle. On the occasion that we scoped her, it became apparent that the dent in her face completely obstructed the scope in the right nostril. She effectively only had one working nostril for the air-intake for her races, and although her resolve was questioned, it certainly offered some explanation for her running style.

Chapter 11

Smile Pleeze

Smile Pleeze had run four times over hurdles in 1997 then point-to-pointed in the Wessex area for two seasons. He won twice before being purchased by Mike Daniel to race for Sue Troughton in the West Midlands Point-to-Point area. He raced for five seasons winning Open races before arriving at Eastnor in May 2004 to run under Rules at Worcester racecourse's summer meetings. He was a twelve-year-old with a handicap rating of 90. His first run for us was a good third at the owner's local track, followed by a hat-trick of wins at Worcester before a famous victory at 16/1 in the amateur riders handicap chase at the Cheltenham November meeting on Countryside Day. I supplied this owner with some of the best winners and days of her racing ownership and she jumped ship because my horses were too thin. They ran well, held their form and having heavy horses running on fast summer ground is a sure way for them not to last very long as a racehorse.

Rock On Rocky (this is me!)

Jan Johnson arrived on the scene as an owner recommended by Charlie Poste, who rode most of my runners at that time. Her horse Rock On Rocky arrived as a five-year-old in 2013 having done some pre-training. He was home-bred in Swansea by Terry Harmon, who had joint-ownership. He proved to be a loose cannon as a young horse: steering was always a bit random, as was his jumping-off at the foot of the gallops. He showed remarkable ability to flail his head around so much that he threw himself completely off balance, but somehow still remain upright and cantering. But once he completed his initial learning process of galloping alongside the other horses of Eastnor – sandwiched between two horses – he proved much better and happier going out solo.

He ran 22 times over hurdles, often blazing the trail which Jan Johnson (JJ) loved. She always felt horses were safer making the running, and keeping out of trouble from the rest of the field. He made the running to win two handicap hurdles in November 2014, and he ran his heart out to get pipped by half a nose at Uttoxeter in March 2015. When his form tailed off, we tried various trips over hurdles at the owners' request, and made all sorts of tack changes, until Charlie Poste recommended a wind op. Although he didn't make a noise galloping at home or in races, he was clearly distressed at the thought of racing. He started being reluctant to load onto the lorry, and although he never actually refused to start I was always on hand to keep him going forward and away from the other starters.

By this time we were chasing. After the wind op, it seemed to take about five runs before he realised he could breathe again, and was happy to load and start after that. He proved also to be, yes you guessed, a Slow Two Miler.

A conclusion that I often have to explain to owners that if I can convince them to try running the horse over two miles they generally finish closer to the winner than over longer trips. Even though jockeys (when they don't know what to say) advise trying further.

Down to a winnable handicap mark with Stan, my son, claiming a seven pound weight allowance (which is allocated to young jockeys to give horses a chance when boys are riding against men), Rocky hit form with a hat-trick, winning three times in one month at Uttoxeter, Ffos Las and Sandown. He won at Newbury and was beaten a short head one day at Ascot. He had a significant fan club following due to his catchy name and flamboyant front-running style. This was amplified by his photograph appearing on every billboard advertising Cheltenham races, laughing in the winner's enclosure. He was on the digital flashing billboard on the M5 flyover at Birmingham, and all over the London Underground tube stations.

In his purple patch, he won off a mark of 130, and ran as a proper Saturday horse every fourteen days in the core season, winning prize money. He retired, sound, after 59 runs, with barely a vet's bill. He had seven wins, ten seconds, seven thirds and ten fourths. That's 34 times appearing in the first four, winning £101,000 in prize money. Once again we see the two mile theory being proven: this long, busy racing career was possible from Rocky because the less extended trip allows horses to last longer and recover faster between races. He was a very special horse who took us everywhere, and JJ – who never was able to watch the horse actually run – consistently maintained that the horse returning safely was first priority, win or lose.

Honeybed Wood

Honeybed Wood was a flashy chestnut mare, bought privately for £1,500 for an owner called Mike Drake. She had a very low rating of 69, previously managed by someone who never trained a winner. On her first run for us we had her extremely wound up, and she finished second at Hereford. She probably didn't have a great ride from the jockey, who certainly knew which horse was supposed to win. Next time, with Richard Johnson up, she absolutely bolted up in a seller. She was a funny shaped little mare, and if she had too much condition on her she wasn't fit. I have to confess on plenty of occasions her appearance didn't make me proud; she was only at her best when extremely skinny. That summer (1997) she won three times in three weeks at Worcester. She won over two miles with AP McCoy, 2m4f with Leighton Aspell and over three miles with McCoy again. She was the Queen of Worcester for 19 days; it was a fair achievement on rock hard ground.

She also won at Bangor with Richard Dunwoody on board. She was very unlucky not to have won a sixth race at Hereford, with AP on her well in command. She blundered at the last, carrying top weight, didn't recover in time and just got pipped on the line.

Swings and Strings
Swings and Strings was an ex-Arthur Moore horse. I can remember viewing him at Dereens and dismissing him because he was the most dip-backed horse I'd ever seen in a thoroughbred. He had been running exclusively over three miles in Ireland, in point-to-points and under Rules, and eventually ended up winning a selling chase at Chepstow. There was no bid for him at auction, probably because of his shape. His connections didn't want to take him back to Ireland, so Will Gaskins, a local owner, bought him and sent him to me to train. We applied a tongue-strap for a run and had another win at Chepstow again over three miles before dropping him back to two, where, making all the running, he won a chase with only four fences as the rest were omitted for fear of horses being unsighted due to low sun. The race was sponsored by a lap-dancing club in Stoke-on-Trent, and the winner's podium featured some off-duty staff and a big black minder!

RUN ON SOFT GROUND THEY SAID! An example of unlucky in business.

Patricks Park
An Irish connection phoned me and asked if we could have a horse to run a few times on soft ground to get its handicap mark reduced to a 'winnable' level. The owners had the belief that the UK handicapper was quicker to lower ratings than his Irish counterpart. 'Just run it on soft ground,' they said, 'It hates soft ground.'

Oatis Rose (Red & Green sleeves)

Burning Truth

Allez Toujours winning at Uttoxeter, 2004

Munlochy Bay winning at Cheltenham, 2010

Rock On Rocky and Jan Johnson

Cool Bob (no. 8)

They were good payers, I'd had a horse for them before and any paying horse is welcome for business at my level. Patricks Park's form wasn't anything special but he had won a fast ground summer chase at Roscommon. The said horse arrived looking very thin and although fit seemed very washed out. We did zero work with the horse and waited for some rain to turn the going soft.

We went to Stratford for a first run and jocked up a young amateur rider. To be fair the owners said several times that whatever happens the jockey must not get himself in trouble. Patricks Park finished a non-impressive fourth. We still did zero work with the horse and he began to freshen up and have a skip in his step and Nicky, his main rider, started chirping that she thought he was a good horse, and she is not usually far away. Next we went to Ffos Las on a filthy wet day. Ground nearly unraceable and inspection only just passed. 'It's soft,' I thought, 'Can't possibly run well.' The *Racing Post* pundits questioned why I was running a horse with fast ground form in such conditions. The stewards interviewed me pre-race with the same question about my planning. I just replied that the horse was unproven and that there weren't many options so we thought we'd just try something different.

A mile out I could see the jockey sitting very still, trying to look around at how his opponents were travelling without being noticed. On bottomless Ffos Las ground the horse won by thirteen lengths with the jockey motionless. The SP was 33/1!

I phoned the owner and relayed the result and it seemed he hadn't even watched the race. In later communications I offered a good price for the horse, on the assumption that the gambling angle had been compromised and it was therefore no longer any good to them. It was frustrating when the horse went back to Ireland. The horse next ran for Willie Mullins over the wrong trip and then turned up at Leopardstown in a €70,000 chase which he won off bottom weight; then he won a similar contest at Fairyhouse as well as coming second when favourite for the Galway Plate.

I messaged the owner, 'And the moral of the story is: it's very hard to stop a very good horse.'

Patricks Park was possibly the best horse to go through Eastnor, but sadly we were not to benefit from any serious prize money or big race glory.

Chapter 11

Allez Toujours

An Eastnor trained winner, notable as the lowest rated horse that I have ever won a race with. At Uttoxeter in October 2004 he won a 0-90 handicap chase off a mark of 58 worth £3,800 to the winner. UK prize money levels only went downhill from there on!
TRYING TO WIN RACES WITH LOW CLASS HORSES AND BEING PUNISHED FOR BEING HONEST!

Cool Bob

We originally purchased Cool Bob in July 2009. He had a likeable profile of Irish form; sound, having had seventeen runs over hurdles and fences, still a maiden but handicapped to give Tony Scrivin some fun. He had a workable handicap mark and was placed a number of times but each time he looked to have fallen to a winnable mark in a winnable race he would bump into an improving type, finish second and edge back up the handicap. Because he always ran his normal game race he was used by the handicapper as a marker horse for assessing other runners in the race. He finished second at Ludlow in November 2010 and returned with heat in his leg. A veterinary examination and ultrasound scan revealed a damaged tendon that would require time off. Tony was keen to have another horse and gave Cool Bob to me.

My son Stan was thirteen at the time and the horse was still only young at seven, so I was happy to give him a home ready to use him as a schoolmaster for Stan when he was sixteen and able to start race riding. We kept him at my mother-in-law's and gave him six weeks of rehabilitation exercise every six months for three years. When young amateur jockeys start their careers, they are restricted to compete in races confined to themselves. To make the step up to ride against professionals they must have attained plenty of experience and be placed or win in their own category. However, amateur races are few and far between and scattered at racecourses all over the UK. The good thing about Cool Bob was that he could run in them all: fences or hurdles, two miles or three.

We had some great days out in our quest to get Stan enough experience; trips to Hexham and Cartmel and multiple other faraway tracks. Good old Cool Bob did his job and usually picked up some place prize money to help with expenses. On his 57th run at Ludlow he finally managed to get his head in front for the first time and win. We retired him immediately. He had finished in the first five 36 times and when he finally won, he collected a huge old-fashioned trophy and a very hearty prize pot. His consistent performance time after time meant he was never weighted to win, only weighted to get beat. Because prize money in the UK is so abysmal it is no wonder that trying to break even via gambling is considered to be acceptable by some participants.

A man with a very small share in a syndicate but big ideas said, 'Matt, there is a horse at Goffs sale (it will make about £20,000). Why don't you buy it yourself and lease it to our syndicate?' Always a good way to make a living – not! Gambling is not compulsory!

CHAPTER 12

JOCKEYS, THEN AND NOW

I know it is not a good idea to live in the past and harp on about how we used to do this or that, but not all progress is for the best. Jump trainers traditionally would have a stable jockey whose main job was to school the horses over obstacles at home and, other than in exceptional circumstances, ride them on a race day. So if it was a busy Saturday and the stable jockey missed a good winner because he was riding elsewhere for the trainer, he would usually get back on the horse next time it ran. There was certain degree of loyalty from the owners and trainers, and the jockeys knew where they stood and remained loyal because they knew that in the long run bread and butter is important.

In recent times with all the data and agents, the rides that have the best chance of winning are identified from comprehensive form. Additionally, there is easily accessible video footage with which agents can assess if the horse jumps well enough for them to make their top clients/jockeys available for the ride. Hence, the most fashionable riders scoop up the cream and the lesser lights have crumbs. The old way meant that more people made a living out of the game. Luke Harvey, the former jockey and now race day presenter, will never claim to have been the greatest jockey, but was lucky enough to ride the winners of some valuable races. Two good winners at Ascot on a big Saturday provided him with enough of a winning percentage to put a deposit down on his first house purchase. That wouldn't happen today, I know.

Professional jump jockeys don't get paid anywhere near enough. They are professional sportspeople and at the height of the season, they could be riding for a fee every single day of the week. Professional footballers receive a silly salary and although they train daily they actually only perform professionally once or twice a week at most. Jockeys can be professional every single day of the week and are followed around by an ambulance. Jockeys have long days: early starts, long distance travelling, race riding and then travelling home. Before the internet and mobile phones, the cavaliers amongst them would travel to the races and their wives wouldn't see them until they got home that night if they had had a good day, hopefully walking in through door in one piece having survived the day's risks to earn a few buttons.

The whole jockey landscape has been changed by the emergence of agents. It is probably the same with other sports, but in horse racing the variables make it a ruthless dog-eat-dog occupation in which survival of the fittest is king. The information available on the Racing Administration website is amazing for keeping abreast of all the data regarding possible runners and riders, and the agents are very good at their jobs securing rides for their own jockeys. However, from first thing in the morning until close of declarations, the last minute decisions of owners and trainers can make Thursday's 'decs' for Saturday cards very interesting viewing.

Even with an established rider jocked-up for a regular trainer on a horse they won on last time out and who is clearly attending that meeting, a certain agent will still be pushing a champion jockey at the trainer, even if your reputation to use the same team of jockeys is an obvious trait. I suppose plenty of trainers may change their minds but it almost seems like a form of bullying. The Racing Admin website has added to the mix by allowing insight to the whereabouts and availability of each. In previous times I would phone up an owner with a list of available jockeys mainly who I had used before and suggest my recommendation and job done, now the data rules.

Aside from all the abuse thrown at jockeys on social media I think the agent situation is the biggest factor affecting jockeys' mental health.

In this day and age when it seems trendy to show concern for everyone's mental health I feel that agents' contribution to the jockeys' welfare is considerable. The agents always blame the trainers but the trainers are rarely sat in front of their Racing Admin site until 10 minutes before close of decs to assess the ever changing jockey availability landscape. The National Hunt agents are few in number and each has multiple riders. Flat racing is different with more agents having less riders on their books and it is disappointing how one particular agent has managed to get in a position of power. It is more disappointing that trainers, jockeys and the BHA have allowed him to do so.

Another recent development during and post covid is the removal of racecourse saunas, supposedly to improve jockeys' mental health. The consequences of this ill thought policy is that hungry young jockeys are smoking much more. So long term health problems are OK but having a daily sweat is not.

In my years of training, 50 different jockeys have been lucky enough to steer me a winner including AP McCoy, Richard Dunwoody, Richard

Chapter 12

Johnson and Paul Carberry: the first three were champion jockeys. There were also many one-win wonders including Owen Burrows, who then went on to train a large string of flat horses in Lambourn for Sheikh Hamdan, and Grand National-winning rider Tony Dobbin. Roger Varian, the Newmarket flat trainer, rode one for me as a conditional jockey at Hereford and when I met him recently he reminded me of the fact.

Richard Johnson was riding a horse called Margi Boo at Towcester and the owners were trying to insist that the instructions were to be to hold the mare up (as in not up with the pace) which clearly was not the best tactic to employ when anyone with any race knowledge could access the form, and taking all her previous runs into her account could see that was not the best way to ride her to win. I gave Richard the heads up about the owners' thoughts and the jockey arrived in the paddock, agreed with their instructions and declared that he was going to 'hold her up in front' and proceeded to jump off in front and make all to win.

Most of the time I tried to use an under-the-radar jockey who was not attached to a big yard. This way it is possible to build a more personal relationship with them, and they can become a regular rider with whom we can have some continuity and rapport. It is hard enough to keep it up. Some owners will demand the best available every time regardless of consistency.

I think it is harder for jockeys with their short careers than it is for trainers. Jockeys have to avoid injury and it is so easy to fall off the radar and a comeback is very tough. Trainers always go through highs and lows, bad season, bounce back, new owners, lose owners, one good horse (we won't go there again).

Jockeys are between a rock and a hard place. If they try too hard and make overzealous use of the stick they get penalised; banned, fined or both even if they win. If they don't try hard enough they receive tougher punishments. The view that the punters can see in their armchairs is very different to the views that the race day stewards make their judgements on. The feel that the horse gives the jockey at any particular time in the race cannot be described or proven for the jockey to justify why he/she decided to make that manoeuvre at that particular time in a race. Was the horse taking a gulp, was there a gap, was there a patch of quicker ground which caused the horse to come back on the bridle. There are so many variables.

There is an apocryphal story of jockeys taking advantage of a speciality bookmaker bet without doing anything too dodgy. The bookmakers have a spread betting market on the aggregate winning distances at every meeting every day so without manipulating the result there was an angle that they could control to their advantage. The jump jockeys would identify a small meeting with few runners and nominate it to be a short winning distance day or a long winning distance day. So the bare result would be correct, no placings manufactured, no horses stopped from winning, which is the worst sin ever. Anyhow on one such day the senior jockeys nominated a short day and connections bet accordingly and all the weighing room who needed to know were on board, except one young amateur or conditional jockey whose mount clearly wasn't considered good enough to be in the shake up. It's horses racing of course, so most of the time anything can happen. The young jockey hit the front and proceeded to win by as far as he could and scupper all the wagers. Fingers burnt. I'm fairly sure it was just within the Rules but harder to manipulate than one might imagine.

Stan was named after a likeable horse called Stanford Boy who although a point-to-pointer of average ability had a character like no other. He would often squeal with delight, loved his work and was a real favourite. He was one of the most memorable horses to have been through our yard. If he had been born a girl he would be named Rose after Oatis Rose.

We are lucky, and Stan is lucky for his parents to have been in a position to help him on the road to be a professional sportsman. Stan has plenty of natural ability and it hasn't been hard to promote him to our owners as first choice jockey. Being a success as a jump jockey needs a lot of dedication, a lot of luck and although if a lad is good enough they will make it even a small leg up that we have provided for Stan was an enormous help. An illustration of this; Sam Twiston-Davies and Aidan Coleman both celebrated 1,000 winners at the same time but Aidan was four years older and didn't have the backing of a large string trained by his father. The same is true of the Bowen brothers; they would have been a lot slower establishing themselves without their father, as would Jonjo O'Neill junior.

Stan was always a natural rider, mainly from his mother's side. After his hunting and pony club experience he progressed to pony racing winning on his first ride at Barbury Castle, beating a Twiston-Davies no less. He was only nine years old. To be fair his pony racing mounts were a fairly average bunch but valuable experience was gained in preparation for his point-to-point induction. That didn't go well. We had purchased a horse called Power Packed Jack from Nigel Twiston-Davies. A fairly moderate

Stan helping me build the yard

beast, but we had him primed for the novice riders race at Barbury Castle. The horse looked to be running the race of his life, hitting the front before head-butting the fourth last and turning a somersault. Stan was ambulanced off, shaken but unbroken. The horse went to Bangor next and won in a close finish. Perhaps the task was eased by the omission of several fences due to the wet conditions as fencing wasn't the horse's best talent. Not the best student at school, we managed to get Stan a job before he was seventeen with Paul Nicholls in Somerset and he spent three seasons at Ditcheat with the champion trainer. During that time he rode ten winners, including at Cheltenham, Ascot and Aintree three Saturdays in a row. At the end of a lucrative conditional jockey season, he was driving a Mercedes and had a WAG girlfriend. One day he called me up. 'Dad, Dad I've got a five grand tax bill.' 'That's good", I replied. 'How many of your schoolmates earn enough money to pay that much tax?' 'None.' he said. 'How many of your mates drive a Merc?' 'None.' 'How many have loads of student debt?' 'All of them.' 'Have you got the money to pay HMRC?' 'Oh yes,' he said. 'What's the problem?'

To date he has ridden me 69 winners and is as fit as any jockey, taking it very seriously having sessions with a personal trainer twice a week. There is no doubt that fit jockeys can take the daily wear and tear much better. The falls are taken better and the recovery is quicker although they are monitored much more closely by the medics than in days gone by. Concussion is more understood and the stand-down times are designed to ensure that no jockey is allowed to resume too soon. There is also injured jockey insurance, which reduces the temptation for a return to the saddle before they are back to full fitness because they need to be earning riding fees. Stan is also sensible about his minimum weight. He has set a realistic low weight which he can maintain, feel healthy and not put himself in the horrible lifestyle of feeling hungry and bad tempered. Modern jockeys in modern times.

The main 'problem' with Stan is that he makes a lot of his mounts look a lot better than they are, and when his post-race analysis is less than upbeat his assessment is usually spot on, which when the owners are delighted with their horse finishing a remote fourth takes the gloss off. It is like many occasions when a horse is in the last chance saloon, having 'one more run' before moving it on it will often manage a fourth place to save itself from oblivion!

Chapter 12

I like to ask jockeys if they have been beaten on a horse by maybe not far that if they rode the race again would they have employed different tactics. It is still very hard to explain to some owners pace and speed and how the race may have panned out with certain pace at certain stages of the race can make a big difference to the cruising speed and finishing positions of certain individual horses. Races that start fast and finish slow tend to be overall slower than races that do the opposite.

Jockey excuses:
'This horse is suffering from LOFTs disease! Lack of fucking talent.'
'I never did like that starter.'

CHAPTER 13

STAFF

I have always tried to give everyone a chance. People apply for jobs and I usually say, 'Yes, have a week's trial.' Some make it and stay while others last only a few hours. Sometimes a really good person may start and you think to yourself, 'Wow, this person is great!' and they last no time at all. Next, a really average person turns up, you spend a week rolling your eyes and all they do is try hard, improve and learn, and fairly swiftly become a key, reliable member of the team and generally stay a long time – which makes me very proud. Mentoring staff has always been crucial in this industry and I like to think that very few members of staff have left under a cloud. Indeed, we treat them as equals as much as possible and never expect them to do a job we wouldn't do ourselves.

I think the member of staff who I trained and has become the most recognised is Ben Delmer. Ben turned up at Dereens one summer when he knew Arthur was away on holiday and said he would work for free for a week and next time we were looking for staff could I put him forward for a job. Ben worked hard for the week and although he couldn't ride he learnt yard duties very quickly and was a nice person to have around. He disappeared when Arthur returned but when we started to get busy at the end of the summer Ben came back, mainly mucking out and yard duties. As a typical Irish way of teaching people to ride we legged him up on to a quiet horse and set him off riding round and round in circles on the yard. He progressed to quiet roadwork and on to cantering. Great! One day he asked me if he could go racing to lead up and I told that he would need to learn how to plait. I set aside fifteen minutes to give him a lesson and he spent every available moment honing his skills until he was proud to show me his excellent plaits. He later went on to be a travelling head lad for Arthur and now is the main travelling man for the powerful Willie Mullins stable.

At Eastnor we have employed some rare folk.

A young guy called Alan arrived on a train having come over on the ferry from Eire. He couldn't drive, had the wrong mobile phone network for our area and through no fault of his own was very thick. But put him on a horse and he could ride anything. He sadly wasn't what we were looking for, as we couldn't risk leaving him in charge. Whilst we were waiting for him to

Chapter 13

move on, his mother phoned to give him a message that the result of his blood test was negative. At evening stables I relayed the news, not really thinking it was any of my business. He informed me that he had been to the nightclub at Kinnegad in County Meath and had unprotected sex with some tart and was worried he might have contracted AIDS.

One particular girl we nicknamed Spooky was convinced she could talk to horses and that they could talk to her. I was fairly sceptical until one day out on exercise she asked me if I had injected a horse that she was riding. I replied that I hadn't and she told me that the horse had told her that I had hurt him. It was true that I hadn't injected the horse but I had taken some blood for testing and there was no sign of any blood or inflammation in the jugular where the needle went in. She also used to tell me that undead people would follow her out of Tescos and get in her car looking for help to pass to the other side.

One of many staff we have had over the years was Lizzie. A lovely, blonde smiley girl. She was mainly part time at weekends and school holidays and then was full time for a couple of years. She was a very keen polo-cross player which is a form of lacrosse on horseback. Once, she requested a weekend off to compete in a tournament. Early on the Sunday evening I messaged her to enquire as to her success or not. She replied that she had played in multiple rounds, made the final only to be narrowly beaten but nevertheless had a fab weekend. She ended the message with, 'I'm all naked in the bath right now.'

As nice a thought as it was I was a tad uncomfortable with a young girl sending her much older boss such a message fearing the fallout if her mum got to view it. On the Monday morning riding out I suggested that such a message was very inappropriate and maybe she should delete it. She looked a bit puzzled, looked at her phone and giggled, she meant to say that she was 'knackered' and predictive text had substituted 'naked.'

Lizzie was also the jockey/rider who had the worst injury off any of our racehorses. She was riding a horse called Orient Bay in a point-to-point race at Garnons when she fell between fences on a downhill stretch. In the melée horses were brought down and Lizzie suffered serious crush injuries to her chest and was very poorly in Hereford Hospital's Intensive Care Unit. I went to visit her shortly after she was taken out of an induced coma and I cried with relief. Lizzie went on to train as an ICU nurse.

Confessions Of A Slow Two-Miler

Several years later Mrs Shep suffered a very bad injury from a fall out hunting. She snapped her pelvis beside her spine and was hospitalised for six weeks, being discharged just after Christmas. Up until then, a local employment agency had supplied a Polish lady to house keep for me and Stan. For Christmas, she returned home, and then we had a girl called Cleo to help at Home Farm. She was the daughter of a family friend of my mother's and was looking for a job having just returned from a stint of post-university travelling. Six weeks of Casia from Poland had the house immaculate for Nicky's return just after Christmas.

Cleo, however, was a bit shy of the hoover but an excellent cook and very easy on the eye. She was tall, blond, willowy and very intelligent. She accompanied me to the races on a couple of occasions and loads of people who usually only nod hello came to speak to me looking for an introduction. Mrs Shep recovered and Cleo moved on. Later she was sighted as Dominic Cummings' sidekick in the Vote Leave campaign for Brexit, and subsequently at 10 Downing Street as Boris Johnson's 'Head of the Prime Minister's Priorities and Campaigns.' I wonder if she put her time at Eastnor on her CV; it surely would have sealed the deal. No doubt when MI5 checked my security clearance no subversion was identified.

Cleo Watson and Dominic Cummings

CHAPTER 14

THE OWNER FROM HELL

John Odell approached me in the spring of 2005 about his horse Moorlands Again. I was familiar with his name and colours and was chuffed that he had chosen me to be his next trainer. He informed me his selection was made on my statistics, which had been fairly good recently. Clearly, he had, as usual, a lot of opinions and not a lot of knowledge or realism on the game of horse racing. But nothing new there. Also not unusually, he insisted on riding his horse out himself. He was not a young man, and he had a blood cancer in remission, so was frail and weak. But he considered himself to be an able horseman; the customer is always right!

He had bought the horse privately and trained it himself to run at point-to-points before sending it to a trainer to go under Rules, which was a relationship that didn't last long. Hell, I thought, it was a new owner, with a new horse that had ability. We could fit in with his weekly regime to ride out, he was always a good payer, what could possibly go wrong?

Moorlands Again was not, and never was, a straightforward ride. Four previous trainers agree he couldn't go right-handed. He did however have a lot of stamina, and won two races at Warwick over 3m5f and finished placed on five occasions. He probably should have had three wins but the owner insisted we tried him right-handed at Sandown, the same weekend we had an entry for Warwick over his favoured 3m5f. At Sandown he was well beaten, and the owner blamed the jockey for not bringing his stick through.

The problem with owners visiting to ride out all the time is that they are always asking questions. Usually the same questions in a different form. Odell was an extreme example of this. Asking the same thing to myself, to my wife, to any staff in the vicinity. Always trying to catch you out and trying to extract a different answer to play against us.

Whilst training Moorlands Again, I became aware of a legal dispute over the horse. It seemed that John Odell was suing his ex-vet, who had previously been a friend, over a pre-sale vetting. Odell had purchased the horse privately, subject to a clean veterinary examination, from the breeder Mrs Linda Williams. The horse already had plenty of miles on the clock, having run almost 30 times. The chances of him having an immaculate vetting certificate were quite remote. Alan Walker, the vet, passed the horse on the day, with a note on a slight problem with his pelvis. He reported that it would not affect his ability to race but could be managed with some short term rehab and controlled exercise, before the point-to-point season began several months away. Because he considered John a friend, as well as a client, he failed to record this in writing: probably against best practice rules. A verbal exchange was deemed sufficient. At some point the horse had a relapse of this problem and was out of action for a short time. Odell tried to sue Alan for negligence and loss of use. He demanded an admission and compensation of some kind. Alan knew his liability position and refused. Dissatisfied with this result, Odell pursued a different track in order to get back at Alan Walker. He tried Blackmail! If Alan didn't admit negligence he would be reported to the Royal College of Veterinary Surgeons.

At some point in the past, Moorlands Again's flu jab had missed the deadline. Alan was asked to fudge the date in order to avoid a potential four week disruption to his racing – a not unusual practice back in the day.

Odell managed to prove that Alan was not on the yard in question on the date the jab was recorded as being given, took him to the Royal College of Veterinary Surgeons and got the poor man struck off the Veterinary Register for a year. When the hearing was completed, Moorlands Again was in possession of an incorrect vaccination record. He had to start his course of inoculations again, and Muggins here got fined £160 for passport irregularities. In fairness John Odell did reimburse me some cash for this.

In addition, Odell sent an invoice to Alan's veterinary practice claiming for training expenses whilst the horse needed to catch up with his flu jabs, the cost of restarting the vaccination sequence and included the fine. Alan's business partner visited Odell and thrashed out a settlement which was donated to the Air Ambulance.

Several years later I had a conversation with the indomitable Noel Chance, a dual Gold Cup winning trainer. He told me that Odell had approached him about training Moorlands Again at his base in Lambourn. Odell arranged an appointment to view the yard and discuss the horse. Noel gave him a morning of his time, seeing horses gallop and all aspects of the training regime, including breakfast, the whole experience. Throughout, Noel listened to Odell's views and gleaned some history. At the end of the morning, Noel had formed the measure of man and had the last word declaring in his unique Irish brogue, 'Thank you for considering me to train your horse but I don't think we'll have room next season.'

Chapter 14

Said no trainer ever before.

On the retirement of Moorlands Again, Mr Odell sent us a young Ikorodu Road for a pre-training session. We were expecting the horse back to race, but it was sent to a point-to-point yard in the Cotswolds, where it didn't make the track. Ikorodu Road is a road round Lagos in Nigeria, which has the world's highest death rate per mile. The horse eventually arrived back here in the autumn of 2008. He was certainly a very strong, ignorant horse to ride. Lots of reaching with his neck to pull the reins from the riders' hands, and not much steering. With no-one at fault, as a result of his behaviour the corners of his mouth became raw. As usual, Mr Odell blamed everything except the horse. Mrs Odell demanded, 'What are you going to do to stop his mouth getting sore?' We tried various different bits, but the straight-bar rubber with a crossover noseband to keep the mouth shut was the best option. The disadvantage of this setup is that you have even less steering and brakes. But hey, at least the horse was happy!

It was OK for us younger riders (mainly me) to deal with, because if we did lose control, we could at least steer the horse in a relatively straight direction. When Odell came to ride the horse, we would use our own, more controllable mounts, to influence Ikorodu Road's performance and essentially remotely controlling the exercise. Odell never realised this and instead thought he was the supreme horseman. On one occasion while out riding with Nicky, the horse got a run on Odell and was heading for a tight gateway in a hedge-line. Were it not for Nicky screaming at the top of her lungs for a change of course, Ikorodu Road would have been long dead and broken, for the gap contained a frighteningly deep cattle-grid! The owner rider did have a secret weapon to keep control of his mount. He screamed, 'Whoa, Ernie, whoaaaa.' Works every time! Not!

In Ikorodu Road's first novice hurdle season he finished second to an Alan King hotpot at Stratford, his first time out on a racecourse. For his second run, he came third in a very hot novices' race at Newbury. The owners blamed the jockey for getting the horse unbalanced on the turn for home. He was clearly a talented animal, but continued to be one of the most ignorant brutes ever.

He won his third start at Southwell, ridden by Noel Fehily, who suggested he might be a Sun Alliance horse, which was a prestigious race at the National Hunt Festival at Cheltenham.

The following season, we started back with a run in a good two-and-a-half mile handicap hurdle at Haydock. The owner explicitly told the jockey that

Confessions Of A Slow Two-Miler

he wasn't to use his whip. Ikorodu Road went off as favourite and came in fifth, beaten seven lengths in what was his fourth ever hurdle race. He ran green and a bit lazy, and needed a clatter from the stick to make him concentrate. But Noel Fehily rode to orders regardless; sadly the owner was still unhappy with the result.

The horse's next run was his first time over fences. He finished a good second around Newbury over an inadequate trip. John Odell then decided to investigate the horse's health, and the vet diagnosed a kissing spine. At the time, this was a fashionable ailment for racehorses, which guided Odell's decision to instruct the vet to X-Ray for the condition. Surprise, surprise, the X-Rays came back positive for kissing spine, proving John Odell, the Best Horseman in The World, right yet again. Then followed surgery to remove bone from the touching vertebrae, and some fairly intensive rehab.

During that time, Odell decided to have the horse trained closer to home, so he could keep an eye on him and ride him more to judge progress for himself (and interfere more). So he phoned around various Cotswold trainers for prices, and eventually rang me to say that Martin Keighley was going to train the horse.

This was a crap week, because my good bumper mare Silver Kate was also going to leave Eastnor, because the owner was going to take out a permit and train her himself. So my two potential Saturday horses were gone, which was a big blow.

One of the trainers Odell had contacted in his search for a new trainer was Charlie Longsdon, who tells a good tale about the man:

A young girl had pulled out in front of him at a junction, and in his rage, he followed her with horn blaring and lights flashing. At some red traffic lights, Odell got out of his car and went to the young girl's window, which she wound down to give him a mouthful. Odell slapped the girl in the face, and as soon as the lights changed green, she scarpered. A third car, behind Odell, witnessed the incident and noted his licence plate. He called the police to say that if the girl reported the assault, he would be a witness. Which she did, and Odell was charged and given a community order sentence. I believe he blamed the rage on his cancer medication.

So when Odell was speaking to Charlie Longsdon about the training of Ikorodu Road, Charlie responded by saying, 'Thank you for considering me and my services, Mr Odell, but I'm afraid the girl you slapped at those traffic lights is now my wife. So I don't think that would be a very good idea.'

Chapter 14

During the 2010/11 season under Martin Keighley, Ikorodu Road ran without much success and returned to Eastnor. We ran him on some very soft ground before finally getting a result, with a head second at Doncaster followed by a neck second of sixteen at Newbury. On 3 March 2012 he won the Class Two Grimthorpe Handicap Chase at Doncaster by a short head. There was a stewards' enquiry, so I had no TV credit because the result was not called for some time.

We had beaten the Grand National favourite; it was my biggest win ever! And I have never been so relieved. There was £30,000 to the winner. Mrs Sheppard had a new outfit, Stan had a new shooting jacket, and I ordered a big load of shavings.

Three weeks later he won another £30,000 handicap on supposedly good ground, breaking the course record in the process. That last Newbury meeting of the season has always been very lucky for me: I won a Mares' Final there, Rock On Rocky won there, and it has just always been a good day. I also seem to have plenty of luck at the Bangor-on-Dee meeting on the same day.

We then had a crack at the Scottish Grand National at Ayr. We went off a 12/1 shot, but Charlie Poste pulled him up. The horse was clearly jarred up after the Newbury effort. It is not uncommon for a horse to show no signs of jarring until they are once again put under race conditions. If they are very fit, you rarely need to gallop at home, and a disappointing run at the end of the season is often described as an 'over the top', but I think most of those horses are jarred.

The following season of 2012/13, Ikorodu Road ran in the Hennessy Gold Cup, and finished a respectable tenth out of nineteen. He'd also finished eighth of eighteen at Aintree, and ninth of nineteen in the Bet365 at Sandown.

It was a more disappointing season, but the horse had peaked: his handicap mark was too high for him to win off. He couldn't cut the mustard in these top class races, so Class 1 contests were beyond Ikorodu Road's scope. Quelle surprise.

The horse arrived back in late summer 2013 in good order. Odell made an appointment to visit, and under no uncertain terms, accused me of not having Ikorodu Road fit enough. I explained the effects of the high handicap mark causing him to run in high class races, and ultimately he had run as well as he could, but he just didn't have the scope required at the top.

Odell refused to agree.

I was upset by his attitude, and phoned him that night to suggest that if he was going to put me under that sort of pressure, I wasn't sure we could have an onward working relationship. Odell disregarded this by claiming, 'It was just his way of getting things done.'

In October we were giving Ikorodu Road what we considered a prep-run at Stratford in a Class 3 2m3f race, which he won convincingly. It was a poor race for the money, over a short trip. We were both pleasantly surprised, considering it was the run of a fresh horse on its seasonal debut. Additionally, he was running off a lower mark of 133 due to his fruitless previous season, with young amateur rider James Ridley claiming another seven pounds. So effectively he was running off a winnable mark of 126, on his favourite quick ground.

Subsequently the handicapper raised his mark back up to 140, his second highest mark ever. Odell and myself agreed that the Becher Chase at Aintree, Class 1, over the formidable Aintree fences, would be his next target.

In the week before the race, I took the usual pre-race blood sample that Odell always requested. It proved to be completely normal, actually with an ESR value of 3, the lowest achieved since his previous successful season. On riding the horse out that morning, Odell pronounced the horse 'not feeling quite right'. He claimed he had heard some gulping noises being made during the usual Monday quiet walk and trot hack. For the first time, he requested a tracheal wash, involving a flushing and endoscopic examination of the trachea and lungs. The obtained samples are then tested for bacteria and other signs of infection.

The vet, Mr Harrison, came to perform the examination the following day. In order to expose any abnormalities before the test, intense exercise is required to exert maximum heart and lung capacity. I rode the horse on the three-furlong uphill gallop in the deer park myself, and the horse felt completely normal. I discussed the exercise, in addition to the previous day's blood test, with Mr Harrison.

The tracheal wash results showed no growth, but there were some signs of inflammation from lower airways disease revealed by the endoscopy. This condition is not at all uncommon in successfully competing racehorses and is not considered a concern. In the absence of any available comparative baseline tests, the results gave no reason not to run the horse.

I did not see the physical printed reports myself, but I have always been happy to take the vet's advice on the rarity that such tests are performed.

Chapter 14

Odell seemed satisfied with the debrief I gave him that evening, and the following week, Monday-Friday before Aintree, I rode the horse every day myself. I gave him every opportunity to disappoint me but at no point did I feel that the horse was under the weather. There was no gulping or excessive snorting, nor any nasal discharge. I made the call to run the horse.

I travelled up in the lorry with Ikorodu Road to Aintree on Saturday morning. We arrived in plenty of time, and I walked the course. Overnight rain had, in my opinion, rendered the going too soft for the horse's preference. In fact, with a going stick reading of 5.2, it was officially the softest ground the horse had ever run on. I conveyed this to Odell once I found him in the Owners and Trainers restaurant, but he dismissed my concern with a shake of his head.

Considering Ikorodu Road had practically everything against him: ground, high class of race, high handicap rating, first time over Aintree fences, I was pleasantly surprised to see him complete. He was sixteenth of 22 runners, last of the finishers; beaten 122 lengths at 33/1. Charlie Poste, the jockey who had ridden him for the majority of his runs, reported that he hated the ground from the start.

Odell disappeared after the race instead of coming to inspect the horse in the stables afterwards as he normally did. The racing lead-up staff reported the horse to recover in normal time and had two clean nostrils throughout.

On Ikorodu Road's scheduled day off following the race, Odell came in to ride his other horse Achimota. I offered to discuss the Aintree race while riding with him, but he stated he wanted to speak to me afterwards, in the house. Alarm bells rang as I realised he was extremely angry. I presumed he was angry about the race result, so I said, 'It was the softest ground he's ever run on,' and he replied, 'It wasn't the fucking ground, Matt.'

Back at the house, I retrieved the horse's passport and offered Odell the option to take the horse away if he wasn't happy. But he refused, telling me not to get emotional.

Later that week, Odell obtained the tracheal wash result and insisted he would not have run the horse had he seen the results. Because, after all, John Odell was also a world class experienced vet in addition to everything else.

A few more weeks later the horse showed signs of being under the weather. Following this concern, we took another blood test which indeed revealed a problem. Ikorodu Road was switched to resting feed (high fibre, low protein) and given a period of rest with daily turnout.

In February, Odell came to ride the horse and make an assessment. We agreed that the horse was sick and we would proceed with light exercise only in preparation for a decision on the Grand National entry in April.

Thus, we continued with walk and trot hacking daily, until one day, about twenty minutes into exercise with Odell riding, the horse tied up, a condition that is attributed but not often explained by an imbalance between exercise and protein in the diet. I am confident that any trainer or vet would be able to recall an occasion of tying up which couldn't be explained at any time, and Mr Harrison told me the condition occurred in our case due to the horse being sick, not mismanagement. Nonetheless, the horse left the yard.

About twelve months later, having had no word from John Odell after the Ikorodu Road veterinary problem, he made attempts to contact me. I had no desire to speak with this difficult, awkward and quite frankly despicable man. People like him do not deserve to own racehorses, especially one as good as Ikorodu Road.

I ignored his calls for as long as I could and he eventually made an appointment to visit and duly turned up on a Friday afternoon. We had some general chitchat about recent racing stories and then he sat down at the kitchen table and declared, 'Matt, I am a reasonable man.' He then set into me about negligence and running his horse when I knew it was sick. He wanted me to accept liability for vets fees, wasted training fees, entry fees, jockey fees, transport and he even came up with a figure for lost prize money he would have won had the horse not suffered the setback!

He threw all sorts of accusations at me and then tried to get me to sign an admission and settle out of court. 'You can fuck right off' was my last comment on the matter.

In the following weeks I received notice of court proceedings and endless emails that I'm sure were legal but very threatening nonetheless, trying to bully and harass me to give up and settle out of court. I took advice from some good friends who were up to speed with the law and recommended a good law firm to represent me.

Odell based his argument around his misinformed view that although a tracheal wash had been taken, the bacterial growth test hadn't been processed as had been recommended at the base of the tracheal wash report, which said, 'THERE IS NO SIGN OF BACTERIAL INFECTION BUT GROWTH CULTURE TEST IS RECOMMENDED.' When he was emailed the test results by Three Counties Equine Hospital he failed to scroll down to the

Chapter 14

second page to read that the culture results were negative! When I emailed him to revisit the vets' report and scroll down to the second page – and the vets had suggested he did the same thing – I thought that would be it. End game. However, he was not perturbed. I don't think he took any legal advice and I don't think he read any of my defence, he was that pig-headed and bloody minded. At the time his trainer was Graeme McPherson QC so he had access to legal advice if he wanted to.

On the day of the hearing in Worcester I was fairly confident, but none of my team would say 'we'll walk it.' My barrister had communicated with Odell in the lobby and reported that he had expressed disappointment that I had enrolled professional legal help but I wasn't going to go into a courtroom half-cocked against such a man who would pull any stunt or dirty trick in order to win.

Our hearing judge in the Small Claims Court was an Indian lady with zero horseracing knowledge, which my barrister assured me wouldn't be problem.

In the hearing Odell thought he was in a TV courtroom drama. 'I put it to you, Mr Sheppard, that you only wanted to run my horse in the big race at Aintree to give your friends a day out at my expense.' It was true that I had some friends on board for a day out, but I always did when Odell's horse was running. They were there to support me because being in the man's company was hard work and never a pleasant experience!

He clearly had more courtroom experience than me, but his whole case rested on flimsy non-evidence.

When my barrister finally got him to accept that the bacterial culture test had been carried out and returned a negative result he piped up, 'That brings to the next part of my case. Breach of contract.' If he thought he knew so much about the law he should have known that you can only bring a claim in writing and can't change it mid hearing, so it was thrown out instantly by the judge.

Throughout the hearing I had Andrew Harrison, the vet, giving his evidence, of whom the lady judge took a right shine to. And my good friend Rhys Jenkins, always a good man to have on your side in any scrap.

The end of the hearing revolved around the horse tying up later that month, and to be fair the horse in hindsight probably had a viral infection, but the pre-race tests gave me no reason not to run. At the time I was chuffed with his performance on very unsuitable soft ground.

At the end of the hearing the lady judge asked for our last statements. I just declared that I was always trying my best and Odell tried to claim that his horsemanship was honed looking after animals whilst based in Africa. She then found against Odell on all counts and awarded me £16.90 costs for my return train ticket and Andrew Harrison's mileage from the vet hospital. My barrister had cost me £1,500 but was worth every penny.

Odell put on a brave face and then tried to shake my hand! 'You must be joking,' I said. He tried again and the lady judge suggested he leave. I think it's fair to say he had never lost in court before.

***

'Matt, if I buy a young horse out of Ireland and it doesn't prove to be as good as they say it is on the racecourse, can I get my money back?'

CHAPTER 15

THE OWNER FROM HEAVEN

Simon Gegg first approached me in 1997 about having a horse. The mare he had been sold by another trainer was turning out to be duff and when it arrived at Eastnor we soon proved that there was no hope for it as a racehorse. We bought him a horse called Oakmont to replace it and he ran quite a few times with some good placed efforts before winning a little race at Ludlow. For next 25 years he paid me a cheque every month except for one, which is a small trainer's lifeline. The only month he didn't owe me any training fees I sent him a statement with a big fat zero. He was the easiest, most generous, kind and understanding man to have anything to do with. He always understood that we were trying our best with all the horses at our disposal and that we always did our utmost to ensure that he got maximum pleasure for his outlay. If we could find a race for one of his horses at Ludlow it was always targeted, as he liked to hire a hospitality box and entertain his friends there with a super lunch at his favourite venue. He was happy to take a chance on a cheap horse and his top budget was a modest £25,000. Well, modest in the bigger picture, but substantial in my world.

Asparagus
Simon Gegg once took me to Ireland to view a young horse that his Irish connections were trying to stuff into him. We arrived and in the yard they trotted up the biggest piece of shit I've ever seen, and it moved atrociously. I said to the trainer's wife, 'Have you bought me all this way to see this?' Perhaps a tactical sales pitch! They showed me some other horses in a field, and one caught my eye big time – despite its head-on action not being great. He had never run but done plenty of pre-training, including racecourse schooling. He was already named, Asparagus. Simon asked how much; they named their price, and he paid. I think they threw the crap one in too as a BOGOF.

Asparagus showed plenty of ability from the word go, with some nice placed runs. He then fell three times in a row while he was in contention. While the jockeys never reported his wind as an obvious contributor, we decided to apply a tongue tie due to tell-tale performance trends at home.

On applying the tie, we never looked back. Amusingly he made more noise with the aid than he did without, as the air was more able to flow over his pallet and in a greater quantity.

We dropped him back to hurdles over heavy ground at Uttoxeter, and he bolted up. He won several more chases and was placed several times. One particular Friday during Cheltenham Festival Week, Jim Culloty was booked to ride Asparagus, after he had won the Gold Cup on Best Mate on the previous day. It was a late race and Jim's only ride of the day: he only just made it in time to weigh out. There were no random drug and alcohol tests for jockeys in those days! I legged him up and walked beside him in the paddock. He was a pale green colour. 'Matt,' he said, 'I'm feeling fockin' terrible...' Luckily, Asparagus was at the top of his game, didn't put a foot wrong and Jim was just a winning passenger.

We campaigned Asparagus over two miles until he edged up the handicap. Then we entered him over 2m5f at Aintree over the National fences. He ran a storming race under Sam Stronge, finishing second to the Grand National favourite. Next time out he strangely fell, and then came a tilt at the Welsh Grand National at Chepstow over 3m5f. We were thinking of a Grand National entry. At Chepstow he was ridden by Owyn Nelmes at a very light weight. Ridden to make sure he got the trip, he finished sixth, beaten eight lengths, by one previous Grand National winner and one future National winner. Sadly he suffered an aneurysm after the finish, collapsed and died. It was a very sad day. Asparagus had 29 starts; five wins, eight seconds and six thirds. He won a total of £70,000.

Kerryhead Storm

Whenever Simon Gegg asked me to find him a new horse, I wanted to achieve maximum value for his loyalty. The horse also had to fulfil some restricting criteria. It had to be able to run on a Wednesday, as this was Simon's only day off from caring for his elderly mother. It had to be ideally handicapped to run over both hurdles and fences, and finally be a maiden or novice in order to be eligible for Wednesday races. Simon set his usual budget of £25,000, and I went to the November Doncaster Sales in 2014. I did my usual homework and narrowed 300 horses down to about ten. I arrived early as per the norm, viewed and inspected my shortlist and the only horse that satisfied me was Lot 8. Historically I've always done well

Chapter 15

early doors. Bidding opened at 600 guineas, and two bids later was sold to me for 800. I phoned Simon to inform him of the purchase and asked him if he wanted this one for 800 guineas or shall I spend the £25,000 as budgeted on another horse. He said he was happy to have the cheapie himself! All in good humour.

I returned to the stable to speak to the vendor, and he energetically tried to persuade me to take Lot 7 as a BOGOF. 'We had no bid; I don't want to take it back to Ireland!' I looked at the freebie's form: if he'd had a handicap mark I would have taken the chance, but without one I chose to give it a miss.

At nine years old, Kerryhead Storm had a mixed profile. He'd won an Irish point to point, been placed in bumpers and hurdles, and obtained a handicap mark while still being a maiden under Rules. He had been campaigned over all sorts of trips but had two miles written all over him. He had pulled up twice recently, which is always a worry.

He was a very sweet, laidback and easy horse. He arrived dull and disinterested in life but Eastnored very quickly. He soon joined in with the hoolies during turnout time, and had a party trick during ridden work of occasionally cocking his jaw and seriously running away with his rider. He had an amazing turn of foot when performing fast pieces and would often race past others in the group with his jaw crossed and the rider powerless. He was fairly fit when I got him and as I Like to Run Them, we took him to the first available Wednesday race at Ludlow, Simon's favourite track, where he would entertain friends with an excellent lunch. Race conditions weren't perfect at 2m4f, but it was a good day out for Simon. Kerry pulled up, and jockey Charlie Poste reported 'two miles and a tongue strap next time!'

Two weeks later, on a Wednesday at Taunton, tongue strap on, he bolted up at 33/1. It was my best ever day's gambling. I had quite a lot on Kerry each way, in addition to a £5 each way double at 50/1 with a horse of Nigel Twiston-Davies's that caught my eye running in an evening race at Kempton, also wearing a tongue strap for the first time. It won at 20/1. Happy days! I probably won back on that day as much as I'd lost in my entire life on gambling.

Kerryhead Storm went on to win three more races, earning £24,000 in eighteen months. He was another very Slow Two Miler. Incidentally, the rejected Lot 7 from that day at Doncaster, went on to win three minor races at Cheltenham. It's a funny old game!

Modeligo

Modeligo was bought privately in Ireland from Martin Cullinane. He was a slight, bright bay horse with a nice step. He started out as a nice workhorse, but never showed any form in his races. His first two seasons were disappointing, over all sorts of trips. Eventually, after a very disappointing run at Newton Abbot, we took a blood test. It revealed that his blood differentials were majorly reversed. The differentials in question referred to the quantities of two types of white blood cell present in the blood: lymphocytes and neutrophils. The ratio of these cells to each other serves as a systematic inflammation marker, and can also be a measure of stress. In normal blood the ratio is 60:40. Glen's was 30:70. Horses with such blood conditions – and I have only ever trained two horses in my whole career with one – will not perform on the racetrack. Their work at home will be good; but under race conditions they cannot cope.

Graham Potts, the vet, tried every trick in the book to correct Glen's blood: arsenic, levisole, everything available to try and reboot the liver into producing new cells at a correct ratio. Nothing changed much. Eventually he elected to take a bucketful of blood – eight pints - from the horse.

When the horse returned to the track at Chepstow in April 2015 after a ten month period of rest he was very well handicapped following his previous bad runs. Application of a tongue strap following signs shown at home meant that he absolutely bolted up. He went on to win a total of three hurdles and six chases; making Modeligo the top winning horse at Eastnor with nine wins. His favoured trip was, of course, a slow two miles. Simon managed to see his final win at Stratford on a glorious summer day but it was his last day at the races before his poor health prevented him from attending.

His outlook on life was always positive and his kindness and generosity very humbling. On several occasions at our staff Christmas party (which has become a society must do on the local festive party calendar) he would make a generous contribution to cover the cost, especially if he sensed if my finances were not in the best of health (like most of the time).

The last horse that Simon purchased was All Good Things. He ran very disappointingly a couple of times shortly before Simon passed away. The executors of his estate kindly paid for the horse to be in training and running for twelve months until bequeathed to me. In that time the horse came down the handicap 30 pounds and won a race in my ownership and although of

Chapter 15

limited ability proved to be a useful lead/work horse and often picked up prize money pay for some expenses.

But the owner from heaven sent an angel….

Tony Scrivin arrived at the yard in the summer of 2009. He was a business associate of Simon Gegg and came on Simon's recommendation. The first horse he owned was called Sarah's Gift, who was a cheap purchase that we ran a few times but failed to win a race with although he was placed a few times. At the time Tony was an overseas director at Spirax Sarco, a massive FTSE 100 company with a worldwide business portfolio. As usual I was always trying to run his horse when he was in the country and available to have a day at the races and see it run. Consequently many of its races were not perfect but Tony appreciated my efforts and was very understanding when, after we sold the horse to Lawney Hill at Ascot, he managed to win three races, which stung a bit. Although they were races I would have considered, in terms of the logistics and finding a race meeting that Tony could attend they were not realistic. Tony then had some fun owning Cool Bob who ran multiple times without winning before going wrong before teaming up with Simon to have a half share in…

Loughalder

Loughalder was a young horse kept in a field just outside of Ledbury by Charlie Hennessy, an Irish pal of mine. He was one of two store horses Charlie had, stable-named Kevin and Perry. We had broken them in and done some educational galloping with them as four-year-olds, which revealed Kevin as a harum-scarum type, always showing plenty of speed. Perry, on the other hand, clearly possessed no speed at all. Consequently, Charlie was not convinced when I elected to buy Perry and not Kevin. But it was immediately obvious that Perry was mild-mannered, keener to please and therefore easier to train.

Kevin did everything at a million miles an hour; he was almost unrideable unless we were really hard on him with a high work load. He looked very light as a result, and I wasn't proud of his appearance. He was also a very unlucky horse. He suffered multiple injuries, a couple of which bought him to death's door. The one day he nearly did win a race, he was beaten by a horse trained by someone who only produced a winner every ten years!

Perry, alias Loughalder, did not let me down in my choice. He quickly became characterised by his infatuation with mud. The wetter and splashier the going, the faster he went (which still was very slow). We had to fence off the brook in the turnout paddock to prevent his daily wallows, which actually caused him to suffer such extensive mud fever that he got it on his head.

He ran 39 times for Simon Gegg and Tony Scriven, winning eight chases and £42,000, and was in the top four 22 times. He won four times at Chepstow, twice at Uttoxeter and twice at Warwick. Jockey Charlie Poste won on him seven times. Loughalder needed soft ground and a minimum of a three mile trip. His wind wasn't great, but a tongue strap helped and following a soft palate operation he won twice over 3m5f at Warwick. He always ran well at Chepstow and I feel this track highlighted the role of undulating going in giving breathers to horses with wind issues. With the soft ground and long trip combined at various tracks, Perry often hit a flat spot. At Chepstow this was at the end of the back straight, after making a mistake at the sixth-last fence. But immediately after the long downhill run gave him a chance to catch his breath, get a second wind and run on to win.

Another Flutter

A further example of a Slow Two Miler was a horse called Another Flutter. He was a last minute wild card at Ascot Sales that caught my eye. A great big ugly bay, nine years old, he was an old fashioned three mile chaser type – or so you might think. Indeed, connections in Ireland had won a three mile handicap chase on heavy ground, and campaigned him as such. Looking at his pedigree and some of his relations, however, I thought otherwise. I had the winning bid at his reserve of £3,500, and was immediately offered £1,000 profit by a northern trainer. We started him off in low grade two mile races over soft ground, and eventually ran him on good ground – or even good-to-firm – and he went from a rating of 106 to win off 133.

In ridden work he was a very slow horse and I thought he had Two Miles written all over him. Sometimes when horses are slow at home people think they are three mile stayers, and are blinkered from trying a two mile trip. If the horse had been younger we may have been reluctant to try him on fast ground due to his size and conformation, but as he was a nine year old it was worth a try. It just proves that you never can tell from looking at a horse's size and shape. His best runs were on fast ground over the minimum trip of two miles at Ludlow, Stratford and Newton Abbot, which are three of the sharpest tracks in the country.

Chapter 15

My son had his first win under rules on him in a Class 2 handicap at Newton Abbot. It was a special day not just for Stan and the rest of the Sheppards but also because the race was sponsored by the Loosemore family in memory of Frank, the father of the Newton Abbot clerk of the course Jason. They were delighted that a small family team had won the race as opposed to Nicholls or one of the other big outfits. Flutter won a total of £50,000 over just two seasons, and did so by running at the same speed all the way.

Hill Fort

Another tongue-strap success story is that of a horse called Hillfort. In September 2015 I purchased Hill Fort at Doncaster Sales, a very laid-back chestnut with a great character, for £10,500. He was nicknamed Hef and started here with a handicap mark of 99. He ran three times with two nice placed efforts and disappointed when favourite at Exeter.

There was no mention from any jockey about wind or any noise, but he displayed the characteristic head carriage that I recognise as indicative of a difficulty in breathing. Thus, I applied a tongue strap as what was now long established as a favourite experiment, for his next race which was a lady jockeys race at Ludlow. Ridden by a top lady point-to-point rider, he bolted up by fifteen lengths and received a sixteen pounds jump in the handicap. He managed another win at Chepstow off 112 and was hit with another rise of eleven to 123, which really stopped us, but he is nonetheless a fine example of a simple stocking making all the difference.

The Bay Birch

We decided to move Hill Fort on and before he went to Doncaster Sales I received an email from an agent called Liam Clark who I had never heard of, punting me a mare who had some form running against another mare that I had done quite well with called Tb Broke Her. Her price tag was €9,000. I punted her to Tony Scrivin and he agreed to buy her unseen. Liam recommended that her best form was on a galloping track, but as yet she had failed to win a race in nineteen starts. Liam was also always a realistic man to deal with, taking only a modest fee. The mare arrived looking very thin and unfit. She was very temperamental to begin with and her nickname soon became The Bay Bitch. She would shoot off in the wrong direction with no steering when she got one on her (which was daily). She did settle down and as she put on some condition she became a babe. She certainly was slow

Asparagus – *courtesy Bernard Parkin*

Loughalder and Charlie Poste

Modeligo, winning-most horse of the yard with nine wins

The Bay Birch

to 'Eastnor' but I was happy to purchase her because of her soundness, her handicap mark, the fact she was a maiden over hurdles and fences and with Tony now retired there would be plenty of races available to aim at. She was beaten first time out at Leicester off a rating of 94 before winning off the same mark at Towcester. This was followed by a second at Chepstow and then a 27 length win back at Towcester before an impressive win up in class at Exeter. Then she ran a good second in a big mares' race at Cheltenham on the very hot day when they abandoned the long distance chase because sudden extreme temperatures in the spring can trigger heat exhaustion, which is very distressing but rarely fatal. After Cheltenham we took the mare to Uttoxeter for a mares only novice hurdle and she bolted up. She finished the season off a mark of 128, 32 pounds higher than when we started.

After her summer break I probably wasn't hard enough on her and she took a few runs to find her form. Two disappointing outings over hurdles followed by some moderate chase runs ensued before Stan pulled her before the last obstacle at Exeter reporting that she made a noise. The wind problem clearly stopped her but unless you hear the noise yourself a diagnosis is hard to fathom. (One day at Bangor a jockey rode his unplaced horse flat out up the chute to prove to connections the roar it was making to account for its poor performance.) Next time out at Warwick we did what we do best and applied the trusty tongue strap. Bingo, she won at Warwick, Bangor and the final of a valuable Mares' Chase series at Haydock in the spring. That day was very warm and at that time of year mares can ovulate and come quickly into season. We arrived at the racecourse stables to witness her winking and squirting. I relayed the news to Tony and gave Stan instructions that if she wasn't travelling he was to pull her up sooner rather than later. Although she was carrying top weight it was a modest contest for the money and she sluiced up, but Stan jumped off her quickly after the line. Concerned, I met her on the course and although she was tired Stan was worried that he was covered with blood that he didn't know its origin. Examination of our mare revealed no wounds so we safely deduced that another mare in the race had burst a blood vessel and sprayed our jockey. She ended the season with a handicap rating of 145, up seventeen pounds. Wow!

Going into our third season I knew it was going to be very hard for the mare. She was too highly rated for the mares-only races and probably not good enough for level weights Listed races. We started in a Class 2 handicap at Chepstow and she absolutely bolted up. It made her the highest rated horse

Chapter 15

to win trained at Eastnor. In the post-race interview with Luke Harvey, he described me as a trainer who 'wins with horses other trainers wouldn't even have in their yards,' which summed up my training life to a tee. She was allotted a mark of 152, which made me very proud. At this time there was talk of a championship race for mares at the Cheltenham Festival and the *Racing Post* had a list of the top ten rated mares in UK and Ireland. The Bay Birch was tenth on the list. What an achievement! Did I get any publicity? Did I fuck! The form of the Chepstow race turned out to be very weak with many behind her underperforming. Only one moderate winner came out of it, the runner-up, who won a race about four starts later. We had a few sniffs from stud managers looking to acquire her for breeding purposes but Tony, to his credit, decided to keep her in training. After all, a race mare like her that can run regularly and pay for herself is a rare commodity. On a personal note TBB became a much loved horse at Home Farm and she has the most character of any horse I have had anything to do with. Her stable was nearest the back door with the big open wall. She whickered when she saw me in the morning calling for a pat and her breakfast, and when she wanted to be turned out, and sometimes just for attention.

In April 2021 we retired the mare. We had had a reasonable run at the Cheltenham mares' day meeting and Tony decided to call it quits. I knew she was still fit and well and had some races left in her but the relief at not having to watch her race and be praying for a safe return above all else made me agree on the spot. 34 runs from Eastnor, eight chase wins, one hurdle win and £100,000 in win prize money. Dr Richard Newland bid us good money and she was ushered away to visit Nathaniel, who is proving to be a top staying sire.

Things owners have said

Gwen Spencer from over the hill briefly had a home bred mare in training. She had a very bespoke set of salmon pink colours which she registered by chance when phoning Weatherbys to enquire about the availability of a pink and chocolate coloured set. The colours department informed her that the plain salmon pink set had just been relinquished and she duly registered them in her name. Roll on 30 years and Weatherbys asked her if she would like to enter them in the bespoke cherished colours auction and after paying just a nominal yearly registration fee, she achieved a bid of £64,000 by Coolmore to add as second colours to their already exclusive plain dark blue first colours.

'I see you have put your fees up! What's that about?'

'My wife had a pony when she was a little girl. She knows about horses.' Always proves to be a tricky situation which generally causes disagreements.

'Matt, if a jockey's agent has accepted a booking and jocked the rider up in the public domain surely that is some form of contract that must be abided to.'

'Matt, I think that if you can improve my horse by 1% in 100 different aspects you can improve its ability by 100%.'

CHAPTER 16

SOME THOUGHTS ON GAMBLERS AND GREED

Gamblers
Good gamblers are traders. There are so many betting platforms to compare prices and value that the disciplined gambler can make a living with tax-free earnings. They need a nice pot of money to start with or a lucky winning multiple to fund the enterprise. In the early days of the exchanges it was not unusual for the top men to turn over £500,000 to make a yearly profit of £50,000. There would be many squeaky bum moments and there are plenty of examples of once well-off punters losing the lot and disappearing off the scene. You see faces whom you get to know and share banter trying to understand their game. At Exeter in the fog on one occasion Roo was in his usual spot down by the second last hurdle when the favourite fell right in front of him. Quick on the buttons of his Betfair account, he cleaned up all that was available from the mugs at home with zero visibility. The point is that he had waited all year for this payday moment, with most days just playing the margins within limits.

One spring evening a gambling friend phoned me, beside himself with excitement. The commentator had mistakenly called the favourite falling at the first fence. Some other trader had thought he was clever to set his liability on said horse at the maximum 999/1. My pal was quick to seize the moment and staked £75, the favourite won and bingo £75,000! Thank you very much.

It was a similar story when an Irish commentator wrongly called favourite falling at the second last and Koo, another 'face', had a £250 at a juicy 999/1.

At Kelso races there is a gap in the hedge beside the road in line with the last open ditch and it is occupied by in-running gamblers waiting for the one moment every year when a couple of seconds pays the mortgage!

Gambling is not compulsory.

Greed
I am not and never have been greedy. My clients pay for service and my occupation of racehorse training provides that service. Some trainers and agents have identified a level of owners who have so much disposable income that they don't care how many people have a cut out of an expensive purchase along the way. They just love to be able to brag how much money

they have and can prove it by being seen to use commission agents to spend their dosh. The more the agents bid, the bigger their percentage. Happy days! These operators have therefore made it very hard for the small trainers like myself to compete.

I do believe that this unrealistic trading is coming around to bite them in the arse. The new money coming through will not stand for the agents wheeling and dealing. If HMRC get a sniff of what was going on, look out! The BHA's review into bloodstock sales practices was conveniently overshadowed by Covid and the agents still have nobody to scrutinise their practices and accountability. The City of London and the stock market have very strict scrutiny from the Financial Services Authority with plenty of rules and lines that mustn't be crossed. Most of the bloodstock agents' tales are apocryphal but a very reliable friend of mine tells a true story.

In a joint venture with a bloodstock agent friend, they purchased a National Hunt store as a foal to pinhook, ie to sell on as a three-year-old. Hopefully the said horse will have improved in size, conformation and some improving winning relatives will make the pedigree look better than when first bought. It is a very common practice in the industry and like most business entails a certain amount of risk. For example, risking a liability of five foals at £20,000 each. To keep for three years and hope that at the end of that time one of your investments is worth £200,000 to make up for the loss on the other four. A not unusual business practice in the industry.

My good friend had a half share in said yearling at 50% of £10,000, paid all the keep and livery expenses for two years and at the end of the deal the horse was sold at auction for £30,000. So after expenses his profit may have been £3,000, which for the outlay is better than interest at the bank and considering he was only relying on one horse for the margin it was a very lucky deal. So far so good. My friend then received a message from another agent claiming to be the underbidder who sent him a vague cash invoice for £2,000 as a charge for services rendered as the underbidder. When my friend consulted with his agent partner in the horse and protested at such a fraudulent practice, the answer was 'you have to pay it, that's how it works.'

OK, I'm not in the clique and have never been on the bloodstock bandwagon. I have no problem with some realistic amounts of luck money being exchanged but the figures being hidden and absorbed by the current traders is obscene and damaging to our sport. It makes ownership and the chance for the small person to have any kind of chance tough, and although there is a massive amount of money being invested at the top level the small people must not be overlooked. We provide the bulk of betting product, which in turn provides the bread and butter revenue that makes the UK racing world go round.

At the end of the day the average punter in the betting shops up and down the country, whose daily gambling losses contribute to the betting levy, funds a huge percentage of racing's income.

Interestingly, in the current uproar about gambling affordability I believe extra regulation would have a lot less government support if we had a Tote monopoly and the state had a bigger financial take out from horseracing, instead of the bookmakers and racecourses.

CHAPTER 17

MY RACE RIDING CAREER (A SHORT CHAPTER!)

No, it's not quite the world's shortest book chapter, but there isn't much to rave about in this section. I failed to win a race until I was 21. Highlights included two doubles at Upton-upon-Severn, four hunter chases and an Irish point-to-point winner at Roscommon. A grand total of fifteen. Although I had a few rides against professionals I was truly never going to rise above gentleman rider status.

I did however ride at Aintree on two Grand National days. The first time was when Hallo Dandy won when it was very wet in 1984 and the second was in 1990, when the ground was very quick. I rode in the amateur chase after the big race. Marcus Armytage, who had just ridden Mr Frisk to victory in a record breaking time, was straight back out to compete with the rest of us lowly amateurs in the very next race and to be fair he was away with the fairies. But just for me to be there was pretty awesome and I managed to finish one place ahead of Marcus in sixth on Chiasso Forte. Nicky had driven from Tewkesbury to Liverpool Airport to collect me and Pat Malone and take us to the races. Afterwards she dropped us off to catch our flight and in those happy days before all the current security checks and because we only had hand luggage we were back in Naas before she got home to Tewkesbury.

Midlife crisis

Nicky had a wayward hunter that we were bringing on. A beast of a horse with an epic jump, but he took a bit of sitting on. We had bought him as a three-year-old from Gill Pritchard and as a four year old I schooled him like a young inexperienced horse for the second half of the Ledbury season, by not overfacing him and preparing him for the future. Without trying too hard I learnt that he was a natural leaper with a good eye. He loved hunting and was a just an exceptional mount. The 2010 Golden Button Challenge is a three mile cross country race on the banks of the River Severn and has become a must-do for all the thrusters in the hunting community. As a five-year-old we entered Fen Edward (named after effing Edward who was effing Gill's husband) to be ridden by Liam Pater, a talented amateur rider and the young horse jumped around safely to finish in mid division.

Chapter 17

Golden Button Challenge 2011 on Fen Edward

The following year I set my sights on competing myself in the Golden Button. I was 45 years old and believed that I had one more fling in me. Nicky made sure that Ed, the horse, was super fit and entered. Pre-race I confess to being nervous but not scared of what lay ahead. On the day Ed was an awesome spin. We jumped off handy but Ed being a half-bred was quickly outpaced by the blood horses. Nevertheless we jumped cleanly away in last place, passing multiple riders sprawled on the landing side of obstacles. I had a mind-blowing experience to finish a very honourable tenth and won a coveted Golden Button for the best Ledbury Member completion.

Ed competed three more times in the great contest. He completed for Nicky's sister Susie, then an unlucky unseat with Ann Bird and in 2019 ridden by Stan he completed to finish the best Ledbury Member for the second time. eight years after my effort. In 2024 Fen Edward is still hunting, will jump the moon and is a huge credit to Nicky, whose horsemanship has made the horse have a lasting career in the hunting field. Most middle-aged men buy an inappropriate sports car, have an affair or embark on some unrealistic quest but my crisis was fulfilled by this unique achievement. I had something to prove to myself, that I still had what it takes. But while I continue to ride out daily I have not left the ground since that day!

CHAPTER 18

MEDIA

How many jockeys and trainers have been built up and up and up, only to be crushed when they fail to live up to media expectations? How many jockeys and trainers have gone from hero to zero and crashed out of fashion when they haven't done anything wrong? Sam Thomas was vilified on decking Big Bucks in the last in a Newbury novice chase. Funny how the connections never ran him over fences again, and he won four World Hurdles. Peter Chapple-Hyam trained two Derby winners in the mid-1990s, had some personal issues, and just to rub salt into the wounds he was entrusted by Qatar Racing to train at the time most expensive yearling ever which turned out to be useless. He now trains a string of a dozen or so in Newmarket.

Lady jockeys of the calibre of Hayley Turner and Josephine Gordon on the flat rode a hundred winners for a season or so then slid down the hill. Hollie Doyle has managed to buck the trend. Henry Cecil went from champion trainer to nowhere to hero with Frankel, who found him, or vice-versa. Sometimes the *Racing Post* prints headlines that make me think it hates racing. Bad news headlines sensationalising bad news. Yes, bad news about horse injuries deserve a platform, but not on the front page! The *Racing Post* is only interested in selling advertisements for bookmakers, and all gambling aspects of all sport. The future of horse racing is bleak. I believe the traditional punters have continued to enter betting shops, while the betting companies make sure there are other ways for them to lose their money. They buy the *Racing Post* at an extortionate price for horse racing, but get diverted by bookies' advertisements as soon as they open it.

If the bookmakers and racecourses carry on the way they're going, there will be nothing for the punters to wager on except non-skilful roulette, online poker, bingo and whatever games of chance the betting companies can come up with to part the stupid from their money.

That will be a sterile, no-thrill existence. No excitement of the first beast past the post, beating the favourite, no thrill of ownership, no thrill of checking one's Weatherbys account to see if the prize money has landed in your account four weeks after it was won.

The horsemen will have bent over backwards, with many at great personal financial expense, to put on a fabulous show on the road, only to be laughed

Chapter 18

out of the paddock. The bookmakers will survive without horse racing but racecourses won't. They have created a spectacle in which gambling has become more important than the horse. A spectacle where the infectious atmosphere of a big race, and even just a little race competition has been hijacked, to create an environment of high-end corporate hospitality through to the rowdy drunken bar, selling alcohol at premium prices, with the real racegoers no longer welcomed. Mainly because they stand by the paddock to watch the horses, or in the grandstand to watch the races, maybe having an overpriced cup of tea and a cake, leaving before the last to avoid the melée. The ownership experience is better, it bloody well needs to be considering the expense of their hobby. The talk about their investment does amuse me. The only outfit that truly invest in horse racing are Coolmore and Co and they ruthlessly make a profit. But once again the Irish thoroughbred industry received a leg-up from friends in government... something to do with no tax on stallion fees until recently, when the EU cottoned on and put a stop to state aid.

I also fail to see why racing can't unite for the best interests of all participants. The fact that there are two competing racing TV channels is absurd. Can't these businesses see that unless they pull together the whole sport is in decline? But the problem is that people who bet and gamble will do so on any sport, whether it be first past the post or who scores the first goal. The bookmakers have worked out that staging all-weather flat races every 15 minutes is the most profitable way to supply the racing gambling product. There must be a big risk that before long there won't be enough owners to pay for low grade horses in training.

What small trainers are up against

I don't know the actual date, but the *Racing Post* started to produce an up-to-date statistics page called Signposts which always makes interesting reading, especially the good form or bad form of certain trainers. The dreaded cold trainer list is the one we all like to avoid. We all find ourselves edging on to the bottom occasionally. I had a winner at Ludlow after a barren spell and a young journalist called Matt Chapman asked why had I been on the cold trainer list for not having a winner for 245 days, to which I replied, 'When you only have ten horses in training it is very hard to have a runner every day.' But, as mentioned before, even when your statistics are good it makes no difference to a trainer's ability to attract new owners.

Confessions Of A Slow Two-Miler

At Cheltenham's October meeting we were in the Owners restaurant and sharing a table with the lady owner of a high-profile horse. We were in conversation discussing each other's runners and hopes for the day ahead. As usual as soon as she introduced herself, I knew exactly who she was and her horses and trainers, she listened to my story and rudely declared, 'I've never heard of you.' I knew that in the previous day's *Racing Post* trainers statistics page that I was miles above her favourite. On this Saturday the paper hadn't included the statistics page, so I couldn't prove my ability or status to her. Some owners are blinded and have no idea of the bigger picture or people like me at the coalface.

When Dan Skelton lost two nice horses on the same day at the same meeting the media all harped on about poor Dan. Yes, it is heart breaking and a rare day of very bad luck, but the yard had numerous horses waiting in the wings and boxes were immediately occupied with paying guests. Eastnor racing lost two horses on one Easter afternoon. At Andoversford Point-to-Point a horse dropped dead under its owner-rider and a syndicate horse broke a leg at Ludlow. Out of a combined total of twenty paying horses in training that was 10% of the string wiped out and neither was replaced.

Also the media sympathises with poor Nicky or poor Paul when they lose a good horse but the consequences for them are minimal.

Bearing in mind how much information and statistics are available to everyone, many of the press have no idea of what is going on. Recently a pundit lauded a young trainer who had a success and labelled him a small trainer. A reference to the *Racehorses In Training* publication reveals that he had 70 horses listed at the time and further research would enlighten the presenter to the fact the trainer concerned's family owned a distillery, a hotel chain and a large chunk of Cheshire, so he had fair leg up in the sport.

CHAPTER 19

HOW TO BECOME A RACEHORSE TRAINER IN THE 2020S

When I started out in life did I even think that I would end up where I am? One of less than six hundred individuals with a BHA licence to train racehorses in the UK.

To become a trainer in this day and age and have any chance of being competitive at anywhere near the top level you need:

1. Start with a large fortune
2. Be from a racing family
3. Marry some cash or have a wife with her own good business or highly paid job
4. Have a serious backer; Bank of Mum & Dad is always helpful
5. Own a farm or some land
6. Have another business or occupation
7. ALL OF THE ABOVE
8. Actually have some talent to train a thoroughbred racehorse
9. To be fair you need serious help or backing at any level to have any chance of obtaining a licence let alone being successful and making it

In times gone by, plenty of trainers set themselves up with a good gamble but cameras and integrity have put paid to that option. Setting a horse up for a life changing gamble is now impossible. Cameras recording every angle of the race means that the handicapper no longer has the bare result of weight carried and winning distance or beaten distance to sum up the result. He can now review the race multiple times and form an opinion of how busy or not a jockey may be at any point.

Add to that, the bookmakers will not accept a serious wager. In the space of a few weeks, I had a bit of luck with some nice each way bets on some big priced placed outsiders that have run from the yard. After one £20 each way bet I placed at 66/1 on Betfair Sportsbook they refused to allow me any more money on at any price. The horse in question finished a nice second and my profit was made, but they didn't like it when I actually withdrew some money from my account.

When I looked at the top 50 National Hunt trainers mid-season a few years ago a quick assessment of names and their status in life made interesting reading. Nineteen of the names would themselves admit to being funded by the Bank of Mum and Dad or started with a large fortune. Six names were from a racing family, either ex-jockeys or a parent who was a trainer. Eight had a major outside backer and at least four had another business. The remainder almost certainly had some financial help which is not obvious. In the top 50 not a single trainer as far as I could see started from zilch. They are all fanatical about horse racing and passionate about their occupation and all very capable trainers, but haven't got where they are today without some form of leg up.

Some tactics employed by trainers to sell their services have over the years been dubious, to say the least, and have soured more than one owner experience and caused them to leave the game. One day at Huntingdon races I was sitting at table adjacent to a well-known but not particularly successful trainer from an established racing background. He was in discussion with the owner of a horse that had not performed very well. The trainer was trying to talk the owner into 'investing' his money in a new young horse which surprise, surprise he happened to have available or knew of.

Some research identified the said disappointing runner and his history was informative. A well-bred individual that cost plenty as a three-year-old had clearly been in training for twelve months before three well-spaced out runs in bumpers, all failing to trouble the judge. The normal trainer line is 'he'll be better over hurdles.' The following season three more poor runs over hurdles. Guess what: 'he'll be better over fence.' Third season racing and fourth year in training for this horse and equally average performances, and now the trainer is encouraging the owner to draw stumps with this horse and try again. The amount of money he has spent and the sum that the trainer has earned has mounted up and the owner has had zero winning or even close to winning experience.

The problem is that the trainer almost certainly judged the horse to be moderate very early on and because of the bullshit fed to the owner about pedigree, conformation etc and it must be good, look how much it made at auction. This man was clearly new to ownership. Established owners who understand the game know that it is a numbers game and expect plenty of expensive purchases will be duff, but this gentleman thought he could get on the bandwagon and have instant success only to step unwittingly into a sea of sharks. Of course there are trainers out there trying their best. like myself, who are genuinely disappointed with a horse that we have been responsible for sourcing proving to be moderate and we try to be as honest

Chapter 19

as possible, often to the detriment of our business, but some people have no morals at all. At the opposite end from a Matt Sheppard Racing experience there have been plenty of new owners who have instant success with a well bought value for money purchase by myself who jump ship the moment the follow-up horse proves to be duff. They usually stay in the game, but to the benefit of another trainer who happens to be flavour of the month.

In my lifetime as a racehorse trainer Nicky and I are very aware of how we have both made our livings and survived without any backing. The only backing we have had is to make it ourselves, mainly by subbing our income through second jobs just to keep paying the rent. The Foot and Mouth outbreak of 2001 made Nicky's point-to-point side of the business very tough, so I took out an HGV licence and drove as a freelancer for local businesses. I also was busy working behind the bar at the Castle for weddings and functions whilst all the time keeping the training show on the road.

The difference between animal welfare and animal rights is TV coverage.

In these ever-changing times of social media, digital photography, long lenses and let's face it the ability to produce fake images to create incidents to be not as they really are, it is no wonder that our sport is up against the wall from the animal rights brigade. Racehorse welfare is possibly as well policed now as it ever has been. There are many standards that have to be achieved and maintained by all the participants. The biggest problem, I fear, is the progress made in the actual race coverage. It is so detailed and close to the action, which is great when everything is going well, but when a horse suffers a catastrophic injury under race conditions the images can be very distressing for even the most hardened horse racing fan. And it gives ammunition to the antis. But most of these people are anti everything. They think animals can talk. Blame Walt Disney for that one. They have an issue with any animal being trained and raced for mainly gambling purposes. Some of these extreme types think that guide dogs for the blind are a breach of the dog rights because the dog hasn't given its consent!

Not so long ago there was a Commons Select Committee enquiry into welfare issues revolving around horse racing and one MP on the panel commended horse racing on its recent success reducing fatalities but asked, 'when can we expect zero fatalities?' which is never going to happen. Different racing countries have a varied degree of what they consider acceptable. America has a lax attitude to performance-enhancing drugs and favour running a vast majority of their races on dirt. In Australia all the runners are examined post-race as they exit the track to see if they have bled from nose and if so, are subject to a compulsory period of being unable to race. If they bleed twice they receive a lifetime ban from racing. There is a story about the BHA veterinary officer who had a grim task analysing the UK fatality statistics. Whilst conducting his research he thought it might be wise to compare his records with those in Ireland and France. The Irish duly forwarded their data but the French were slow to respond. On chasing up France Galop he received a message to say that 'we don't keep any records of fatalities, Monsieur.' But I suppose the French have no problem eating 'chevaux.'

The vast population of the UK have no opinion on horse racing. They are never asked! If, however, you gave them a chance to speak you would have to ask them a leading question. For example about the use of the whip to encourage horses to run faster to win, for gambling purposes or to enhance bloodstock value. The liberal leftie wokey society into which we appear to be subsiding have not yet taken into account that horse racing is about breeding and conditioning animals to be the best and to compete to be first past the post.

Human society has in recent years been brainwashed into thinking that taking part and being last is fine as long as you tried your best. Our society doesn't inspire anyone to be elite whereas the horse racing industry does pursue excellence. Which myself and many likewise hunting, shooting, fishing and farming countryside folk have been brought up to strive for. Whether it be the best crops, the best dairy cows, the best fat lambs. The racehorse breeding industry has peaked as far as performance is concerned. Race times are never going to be any quicker than they are now as human athletes only break world records by milliseconds and they are probably drug-enhanced, but we won't go there.

I never realised until recently what a game changing decision it was when the BBC ceased coverage of horse racing. For years we only had three TV channels and sport content was always competing for space. The left wing agenda of the BBC didn't consider horse racing to be appropriate and it dawned on me recently how when growing up we all trusted the BBC because we thought it was patriotic and true. However, gently and consistently they were brainwashing us and we didn't even know it. Now it is worse, they are trying to ram their agenda down our throats. As far as animal welfare goes the first thing that needs to be outlawed is halal and

Chapter 19

kosher slaughter - which will never happen due to religious beliefs – but keeping horses to race probably will be. And I only have one thought on veganism. When I was at primary schools in the late 1960s, only twenty years after WW2, at morning break all the pupils had a third of a pint of milk to ensure a daily calcium hit to prevent rickets. If these hysterical eco-friendly parents are forcing their children (and pets) to go vegan, what could possibly go wrong?

Not sure that the Paddy Power adverts showing talking horses is a necessarily good angle either. Oh look, racehorses can talk!

I suppose that in a position of being a racehorse trainer I am privileged to know a lot of information that other people don't. I admit that there are plenty of occasions when I have avoided disclosing to the stewards when a horse has a noisy respiratory problem which I think a tongue strap might help, but as I have mentioned before they don't have to make a noise for the application of a piece of stocking to transform a horse's racing form. Or is it that they been so compromised by their inability to breathe that they have handicapped themselves?

All trainers have to be so careful now with any explanations as the professional stewards' secretaries all have law degrees and are making comprehensive notes of our explanations as if we are all suspected of cheating. It is no wonder that the most common explanation is that the trainer had 'no explanation' as to an improved performance of an outsider or a disappointing favourite. At the end of the day we are all doing are best to win races for the people who pay us to care for their horses.

Who are we responsible to? Our clients or the punter? We provide a product for the bookmakers to provide a gambling medium, we provide an amazing first past the post is the winner spectacle for racegoers to cheer and soak up the atmosphere for the racecourses sell as a family day out. The racecourses receive money for every race they stage plus any paying public. For them, pre-Covid, it was a very profitable business model. But the powers that be rely on people wanting to be owners and are willing to pay for that enjoyment. The pool of owners is reducing and new potential owners are harder and harder to find because they just aren't there any more.

It is so deflating when you have an average young horse run well in a novice hurdle and when your elation subsides you reflect on the fact that the handicap mark will be way above the horse's ability and it will take at least six runs before he or she can run in a race with any kind of chance.

What would I have done differently?

I have tried to promote the benefits of training National Hunt racehorses on only grass gallops and have proved time and time again that I can keep horses sound and deliver them fit to the races to win and be competitive. In 28 years only one owner has ever sent a horse away because I didn't have an all-weather gallop. The rest of the owners that have joined me probably didn't ask or realise that we didn't have the use of one.

I suppose as I have aged I have given up on trying to improve my facilities. I feel that I have managed long enough, making do with everything I have here in Eastnor. I have done my best with what I have at my disposal, converting existing barns and sheds into enclosures that can contain an equine animal. Horses don't care what their stable looks like. As long as they are warm, dry, fed and watered. Some yards can be all singing and dancing. In the beginning we made the stable doors ourselves to fit the doorways. Family friend Bill Didcot, who worked at the local coffin factory, filched some 'lovely bit of walnut' coffin planks from his workplace and skilfully made two doors which we hung with some ancient hinges that I scavenged off some rotten old wooden gates that I had spied. We even used second hand screws and hand drills, we had so few funds.

Do you do what's best for the horses? Do you do what is best for the owners? Do you do what's best for your business or what's best for yourself?

Have I failed? No. Have I succeeded? Sort of!

The National Trainers Federation

I was always keen on the political side of racing and always tried to attend regional meetings of the NTF. In time I was asked to join the council. This required attending meetings in London three times a year, for which a train trip from Ledbury to Paddington was a great escape and something completely different. One of the reasons to get myself on the committee was to take my wife to London, maybe for an overnight, do some shopping and go to a show. She only joined me once!

The meetings were some, to me anyway, big league. There were various presentations from racing top table figures. There were some fairly forthright voices and we learnt which agencies disliked other agencies and who didn't get on with who. I always tried to make my case for the small trainer and at race planning meeting I suggested veteran horse races for conditional jockeys which has now become a popular series. I was always chuffed to sit next to John Gosden and always amazed how so many members of the NTF had no idea what was going on in the background for their benefit. The majority just like the all entry metal badge.

Feel like shit? Keep calm and carry on!

Throughout my twenties I had episodes of extreme tiredness and would also randomly get a very itchy rash around my ankles. As I got older the symptoms got worse and on some very busy days I might ride out four or five lots and on dismounting the last I would barely be able to shuffle across the yard. I just thought it was old age but I was under 50. I was working some bar shifts at the Castle for weddings and carrying crates of drinks up from the cellars broke me. It later transpired that there was acute inflammation in my lower joints. After lunch I would set off to do a job, maybe cutting birch saplings for constructing fences and I would sit on the tractor for half an hour nearly in tears trying to summon up the energy to complete the task. Then I would maybe manage half an hour before giving up. Nonetheless, I put on a cheery face and carried on.

It came to a head when we had to manhandle sixteen pallets of shavings off an articulated lorry. I had enlisted some help, led from the front, worked up a sweat and completed the task. The next morning I awoke with a rash all over my body and not very well at all. Multiple trips to the doctors ensued with little diagnosis. At one point I was stood in front of two GPs completely starkers whilst they took photos for their notes. My parents came and collected me and took me to visit a witch doctor-type quack whose special trick was to spin crystals. Without any inspection of my rash he diagnosed that I was suffering from orf virus, which is a sheep based infection. I had originally suffered from orf when working on a sheep farm when I first left school at eighteen.

More visits to a doctor finally got me a consultation in the Dermatology Department at Hereford General Hospital, where erythema multiforme was diagnosed. Online descriptions compare it to having shingles, chickenpox and herpes all at the same time. The consultant said that they wouldn't keep me as it was coming to an end but 'you have been very, very poorly.' That I knew! More research confirmed it was linked to orf and that I had been carrying the virus since my teens. A blood test revealed that at some point I had suffered glandular fever and the canine parvovirus, which is odd because I have never been a dog lover or owner. At one point my limbs at joints were so inflamed that I needed help to get out of the bath. As always Mrs Shep held the fort.

It was a similar story when my right hip finally gave in. My family have a hereditary arthritic hip disorder. My younger brother has had both hips renewed, as has my younger sister and my poor old dad. It is more than possible that my racing lifestyle and occupational falls and graft have been instrumental in the cause of my current bodily condition. I had been struggling with riding for several years when a slight change of routine caused my condition to worsen significantly.

On a busy morning when we had lots of young people riding out my usual race exercise saddle had been taken so I used the only safe saddle left. It was a lightweight synthetic general purpose non-race exercise type with a very high cantle, which is the high arched part at the back of where the rider sits. As I slung my right leg over at my normal/maximum arc it proved not to be high enough and my right leg's trajectory was deflected by the saddle's shape. I fell into the saddle nearly in tears. From that moment my right hip instead of being painful 30% of the time was now painful 90% of the time.

In the following three months I wrecked my stomach taking too much ibuprofen and started rising at 5.30am just to have some toast before taking paracetamol. I struggled on until a late spring afternoon at Chaddesley Corbett Point-to-Point when I walked up and down the viewing bank multiple times and in the end ground to a halt.

That night we went to a local barbecue and I didn't know whether to stand up or sit down. My sister Toni had gone abroad for her hip replacement and using her French agency, Laurent, I put my details on an online application form. Twenty-four hours later I received a quote, a date in three weeks' time and an itinerary of which flights to catch out of Bristol to Nice. The quote, which was pre-Brexit, was £3,550 on presentation of European Health Insurance Card from which the French claimed back the rest from the National Health Service.

I signed up, booked my flights and made the necessary arrangements. I arrived in Nice and was collected by the main man in the Laurent agency and driven two hours down the French Riviera to Toulon for a couple of days of pre-op tests. When I lay on my back with my knees bent up towards me, my sideways rotation of my right leg was millimeters compared with my left which was normal with full rotation but was beginning to ache due to carrying the burden of compensation for the other limb. Nicky joined me

Chapter 19

at the weekend and with the operation on a Monday morning she had five days on a beach in the south of France whilst I recovered.

On the Friday Laurent provided an electric Tesla limo to return us to the airport and had sorted out assisted boarding at both ends of the flight. The procedure was done with access through the front of the pelvis and because I had elected to have the operation done before there had been too much muscle wastage my rehabilitation had been swift and I was back mounted in ten weeks. Although I was plenty young enough for the operation I felt that at this time in my life my fitness and ability to work to the maximum was crucial to my business.

Racing behind closed doors at Leicester

At the Sales with Ed Bailey

CHAPTER 20

COVID-19 2020-22 LOCKDOWN (AND POST-LOCKDOWN) DIARY

29 May 2020: This spring has been awesome for the weather. We've been able to rough off horses to Ed Bailey's farm at Upton Bishop. Last month and this seemed to be the best spring in living memory. The horses have had eight weeks on good grass, nice warm weather and very few flies for the time of year. It was good timing and a welcome highlight in a very testing time for everyone.

In March I'd turned 55 years old and took the opportunity to dip into my pension for £13,000 to clear my overdraft. The government has given us a £10,000 small business grant and we've applied for a further £15,000 self-employed grant. The staff are receiving furlough money and I consider it is a good strategy by the Chancellor for small businesses to be able to resume when lockdown is lifted.

I had some bored young jockeys looking for something to do. I suggested a stone picking session on my natural sand gallop. It had been in place for around fifteen years and for a small rent provides us with a place to safely work the horses when the grass is too firm. Some summers we can be on it for months and others hardly at all. Usually just when I get it level and up and running following a dry spell it immediately starts to spill with rain! Anyhow, on this Covid spring morning Stan, Richard Patrick and I made a start at manually removing all the exposed stones from the sandy soil. We methodically picked our way until we approached the sandiest uphill section and were greeted by a crevasse of Grand Canyonesque type depth! It was eight feet deep with all the sand washed to the bottom of the slope or further into the brook. The heavy rain had penetrated into a extensive badger sett and washed away many tons of sand. The local agricultural contractor was enlisted to make good the damage. The bill has come to about £1,500, but to be fair it wasn't as if multiple tons of expensive artificial all-weather gallop surface had been washed all the way to Gloucester.

5 June 2020: We brought some horses in, anticipating the resumption of racing after the recent hiatus. Owner support has been very good, and humbling.

Not Available winning at Newbury Meeting, November 2021

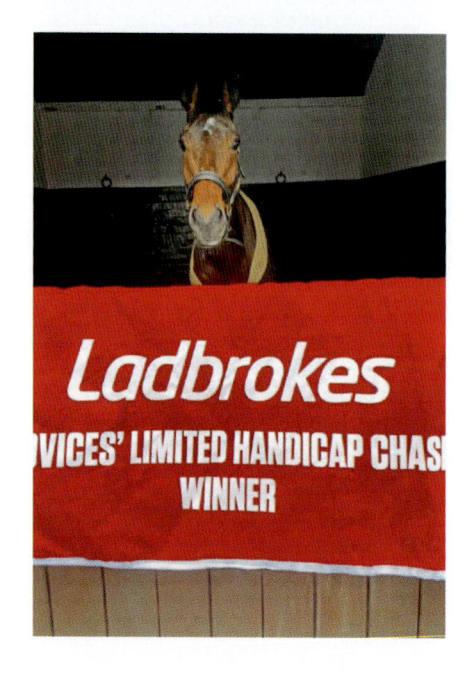

Not the Grand Canyon! Matt Sheppard sand gallop, 2022

6 August 2020: We got off the mark for the post-lockdown season today when Getawaytonewbay (winner number 174) recorded her first win for us over fences at Stratford.

2 October 2020: Things changed a lot! I took a fall from a young horse a week ago. It wasn't so much the fall as the hitting the ground. Dazed but not concussed, I stood straight up. Nicky Esling rounded up the loose horse, saw that I was upright and headed back to the yard to send a recovery vehicle to collect me. It must have been 25 minutes, it was chilly and I was stood in the shadow of an oak tree. I figured that if I could shuffle across two yards I could at least be in some sunshine. My body said, 'Not bloody likely, Matt.' I managed to remain standing until my Nicky arrived on scene with the truck and took me back to Home Farm. The girls helped me into the house and placed me in front of the fire. My wife said, 'I'll just ride another lot and then see if you need to go hospital.' Country folk! We never want to be a drain on the NHS. In an unwise move I attempted to make it to the downstairs loo. I didn't. I passed out in the doorway.

When I came round I still had my mobile phone so I dialled 999. Not sure where the emergency service call centre was based, but the operator had never heard of Herefordshire. She eventually dispatched an ambulance and I called the estate office at the end of the yard to look out for a flashing light. Our very good friend Viv came round from there to check me out and when the paramedics turned up they identified a problem, in that some scaffolding around the back door would prevent the stretcher exiting. So Tim and Bob from the works yard next door rocked up with angle grinders and all the kit to provide access. However, on inspection Bob the carpenter spotted a roll top desk in my office in front of an unused door. Quick as a flash he dismantled the wobbly old desk and there was my exit sorted. I passed out again once on the stretcher, and again when being assessed at Hereford County Hospital A&E.

A CT scan revealed a haematoma between my bladder and pubis bone. Thankfully nothing was fractured and my artificial right hip was undamaged. We had a Covid secure family wedding the next day and I messaged the bride telling her I would be fine to attend because 'morphine is amazing stuff!' I was tested for Covid and wheeled into a side ward awaiting a negative test before being moved on to a ward. Catheter fitted, I couldn't walk for two days and even then it was only a zimmer-frame shuffle. The internal bruise became a scrotal haematoma which looked very much like a black pudding (photo

Chapter 20

available on request). My deteriorating left hip gave me the impression that a replacement was one year closer. I spent five days in Monnow Ward and can only praise the NHS. In an hour of need we are so lucky. Mrs Shep kept the show on the road and Kestrel Valley scored at Ffos Las.

The problem with our occupation is that I hadn't had a serious bump for about five years. Bearing in mind the risks we subject ourselves to every day riding thoroughbred racehorses, I was due a spill. Shit happens!

25 November 2020: Back on a horse after eight weeks. As with most broken horsemen I figured that I could ride better (with less pain) than I could shuffle. It was also an economic consideration, in that to make the business work I need to be hands on. Stan had helped out as much as his job would allow but needs must!

It has dawned on me that my aches and pains are as a result of my horse riding injuries, the falls and general wear and tear which at the time you consider just a 'knock.' I have been ambulanced off to hospital at least four times as a result of falls. Well, it's not the fall but the hitting the ground that causes injury. I turned a somersault at Garnons Point-to-Point when I was nineteen. The horse put both front feet in the open ditch, fired me over the fence and rotated to land on my pelvis. Luckily the ground was very soft and it absorbed much of the impact as the hindquarters of the mare imprinted me into the turf. Hereford Hospital took X-Rays and sent me home, judging that being young my bones still had some flexibility. I was also ambulanced off a point-to-point course when I fell at the last fence on my last race ride. I spent three days in Shrewsbury Hospital with concussion and don't remember any of it. I was scooped up off the road in Eastnor when a young horse flipped over backwards. I was lucky because I landed in a big deep puddle which lessened the impact. After an X-Ray I was discharged. I was also ambulanced out of my bedroom when my back went into spasm.

Other injuries include collarbone, wrist and humerus (actually fell over at a party), fractured shoulder blade (sent home with paracetamol), multiple toes, fractured ribs and a punctured lung. Not to mention countless sprains and bruises that all take their toll in the long run. A last fence unseat at the Golden Valley Point-to-Point meeting at Bredwardine in the mid-1980s caused a shoulder dislocation which still gives me gip added to the fact that as I emerged from the St Johns Ambulance tent feeling very sorry for myself my mother, who wasn't even the owner of the horse I had fallen off, kicked me on the shin for my losing a winning chance.

None of this compares to my wife's short but severe injury list. Ambulanced from a stable after sustaining a broken fibula whilst clipping a young horse and a more serious hunting fall when she was airlifted out of a very muddy Herefordshire field with a smashed pelvis. She spent six weeks in hospital over Christmas and New Year with a consultant telling her that she may never walk again. Little did they know her determination to get back to normal. And her most amazing trait is that no matter how much pain or discomfort she may be in, she never complains, ever.

15 December 2020: Kestrel Valley has ticked a special box to become my first ever winner at Wincanton. I have had plenty of placed runners at the venue but always felt that an outing was venturing into the lion's den of the West Country powerhouse stables. The prize money was a paltry £2,700 to the winner so my quest for £2m is looking unrealistic.

4 January 2021: A new follower on Twitter; a tongue strap sales company. A good try, but I'll stick to using ladies stockings, thanks!

14 January 2021: All Good Things won a race at Bangor on the unraceable type of ground he needs to be at his best. Down to a winnable handicap mark, he duly hacked up. It was possibly one of my worst ever race day experiences, except when losing a horse. Bangor races is always the best day out for owners and trainers. Jeannie Chantler is a top class hospitality manager and owners will often request a trainer to find a race for their horse even if it is not perfect just for a VIP day out. The Bangor and Chester Racecourse Company have an excellent policy to maximise the number of runners by offering first class hospitality. If the races have a minimum of eight runners then the racecourse receive £8,000 for every race, less than eight it is minus £500 for each runner less. Today, under Welsh Covid restrictions there was nowhere to sit down in a dry room; only sharing stables with the runners or sitting in our vehicles. The weather was filthy but another winner was chalked up. The other unforgettable aspect of it was a dose of scrotal shingles (not having much luck in that department), so feeling a bit down and a chilly damp afternoon did me no good.

21 January 2021: An unexpected development was an approach by David Dennis to team up and train his horses with him after he had a parting of ways with Tom Symonds. I have known Dave for many years; he was my main jockey for a couple of them and rode me sixteen winners. Following a messy divorce and subsequent developments he found himself with nowhere to train. His venture with Tom had been very successful in terms of winners

Chapter 20

but the relationship broke down, so when he asked me I was happy to provide him with a base. Dave is bringing thirteen fit horses with him, several of which have recent winning form. As with all partnerships you need to work hard to make a go of it, but knowing Dave as I do, he does; his life has been upside down in recent years so some Shep stability should be useful to him.

It also means my quest for 200 Eastnor-trained winners will be boosted by some of Dave's horses winning in my name, You never know, that £2m prize money target might just be within reaching distance. The timing of this union may be considered fortunate by some as I had no choice in the present world economic and personal circumstances, but I was under little pressure. When I met his owners who were supporting him I was humbled with their loyalty and praise for David and his honesty, and how they appreciated his work ethic and communication skills. I am happy that we should work well together and am looking forward with a skip my stride to enjoying being busy in the sport I love. That is something that is very hard to maintain in any walk of life, to keep up enthusiasm through thick and thin. My stale cynical outlook needed a boost and maybe sharing some success with David would be just the ticket.

This week also coincided with some good news about business rates. Christopher Marriott, the National Trainers Federation ratings advisor, had contacted me earlier in the year to offer his services to appeal my property valuation. The Valuation Office Agency had put a rating value of £550 per stable on my premises on the assumption that every race horse training establishment was on a par with Newmarket, Lambourn or various other purpose-built palaces. My stables here at Home Farm are certainly not up to that standard. Mr Marriott's appeal was successful and my rateable value was reassessed below the threshold of having to pay £3,500 per annum to zero and we can also claim a rebate of payments dating back to 2017, which in total are £10,500. The timing was good, as my tractor needed a £5,000 birthday present.

An observation in these troubled times is how many trainers who consider themselves to be elite and superior are happy to accept any horse to train regardless of its lowly handicap mark. Many of these trainers are the same ones who look down their noses at trainers like me who dare to invade their territory on the rare occasions we have a horse worthy enough. Welcome to our world!

20 February 2021: A very mixed week here at Eastnor. It began with Monday morning when Jodie received a kick on exercise and broke her tibia. She was at the bottom of the short gallop, which was very soggy, but luckily when she came off she managed to be sat in the only dry spot. I called 999 and awaited response vehicles to arrive. The call handlers always ask if the horse was moving and during the pandemic asked if we could be wearing facemasks when the ambulance crew arrived. That was a big ask, as we were in the middle of a field in very rural Herefordshire. Jodie's boyfriend arrived in a 4x4 pick up and we scooped her on to a stretcher and on to his vehicle to cross the field, towing it to the main road with my tractor because it was so wet and thus to the awaiting ambulance. The air ambulance was fogbound at Strensham. Later in the week David had his first Eastnor winner when Hardy Articos won at Hereford at 50/1 and on the Thursday The Bay Birch returned to the winners enclosure after an eighteen-month absence. It was a long time coming to the mare, but all her contests were hard as she was forced to compete in races that were beyond her class due to the unrealistic rating she received for winning at Chepstow.

23 February 2021: As usual the handicapper overreacts and The Bay Birch gets another seven pounds lumped back on for winning a four runner mares only at Leicester.

4 March 2021: Broken Quest scores at Ludlow. Team ShepDen have crashed into the top hundred trainers and it always fascinates me to view statistics and compare myself with other trainers, many of whom have much more resources and backing than Matt Sheppard Racing. The number of winners to number of horses is relevant, and the internet can provide access to information about how much the horses have cost to win so little.

20 March 2021: Cheltenham fatalities have been low because of Covid; no crowds means no social runners.

25 March 2021: Just hit 56 years of age. My birthday appears in the daily column of horse racing's great and good list in the *Racing Post*. It is usually a day friends send best wishes or banter to help celebrate your day (or not). Today WhatsApp was silent, which suggested to me that most racing professionals do not buy the overpriced over-rated rag that glorifies bad racing news and gambling over our sport and passion.

3 April 2021: Innisfree Lad was winner number 180 for us at Haydock. Richard Johnson retired at Newton Abbot today. He was hoping to go out at Hereford the next day but ground concerns forced the meeting to be

Chapter 20

abandoned. A fine example of a sportsman and a person. Dedicated, honest and humble, win or lose.

20 April 2021: We've retired The Bay Birch in one piece after her final run at last week's Cheltenham meeting. I was relieved when Tony Scrivin made the call. The mare meant so much to me and had been such a mighty character that I was always feeling sick each time she ran, fearing for her safety. Tony has no interest in breeding from her himself so we accepted an offer from Richard Newland who will send her off to visit Nathaniel, the sire of that awesome flat race mare Enable. We are all looking forward to seeing her offspring on the track.

Lorna Brooke has died after a fall at Taunton earlier this month. Her death needs to remembered by a celebration of her love of her racing life. Not a social friend of mine, but a regular smiley face whom I will miss a great deal as will many in our sport. A closer friend, Richard Davis, was also lost in 1996.

16 May 2021: Risk And Roll won a two-and-a-half-mile point-to-point at Tabley in Cheshire. It's Eastnor's 162nd winner between the flags and the first in a while, as the sport had been disrupted majorly by Covid – as had so many. The local councils had a big say in allowing fixtures to go ahead and it only took one anti-horseracing councillor to make it very awkward for the organising committees to stage a meeting. How there was any significant danger of catching Covid in the middle of a field is beyond sense. However at the Ledbury meeting staged at Maisemore Park in October 2020 the police turned up with drones to catch any gatherings of more than six people!

1 May 2021: Cyclop won last week's Highland National at Perth under a champion ride from Brian Hughes. Now, at the end of the season, statistics had the team as rated 81st on the trainers' table with £107,000 prize money, above trainers who had run many more horses and only £7,000 behind a trainer who had run 88 individual horses. Do people look and identify our success? What do you think?

A very dry April ended with many winter horses having end of season runs resulted in a higher than usual number of fatalities than normal. Cheltenham and Aintree had been thankfully low in equine casualties, so elsewhere was a wakeup call. As usual the BHA overreact and declare a pre-race trotting up of all runners at last-minute selected jump meetings. The racecourses and bookmaker want summer jumping and trainers supply the product but as usual they seek to blame the trainers for equine deaths, not the courses for skimping on groundsmen or watering. Although my business module has been built around summer runners at the local tracks I am fairly sure that annual fatalities would be much reduced if summer jumping was banned. That is not to say that the courses have done an amazing job improving their irrigation to provide safe ground, it is just the nature of the beast is not best served by an artificially prepared surface.

5 May 2021: The new season kicks off with Schnabel winning for the second time for us at Fontwell. David's horses have improved again, but the handicapper may have a say.

21 May 2021: Always Able was a very special winner at Stratford. Simon Gegg's sister Veronica had gone into partnership with Marcus Jordan and the mare won in Simon's colours. An easy partnership to deal with; their colours are alternated for each run.

In view of recent revelations and speculation over drug misuse in the Irish horse racing industry it strikes me as notable of how keen Willie Mullins is to source new blood from the UK point-to-point field.

24 May 2021: Cadie returned from Ludlow races delighted that she had won her first best turned out cash prize of £30. I recalled the memory of the only time the Matt Shep plaiting and grooming skills secured a best turned prize of £50. I led up Divine Charger to win at Ludlow in 1987. It was a week's wages at the time and I wrote a thank you letter to the sponsor, but let's face it, 34 years ago, that is not a fact that British racing should be proud of.

17 June 2021: Kalinda wins at Uttoxeter. We acquired her from Ireland with a hint of ability in bumpers on good ground and with no serious skulduggery managed to get her handicapped at 85. Fast ground on the day proved ideal and under a fine ride from Stan won by a neck at 16/1. I think that the win was the first time that I have won with a handicap debutante. If you run a moderate novice too honestly you always receive an initial mark that is unrealistic and unwinnable off. My job description is to train racehorses to win. If it was to train horses to run to their best every time I would train fewer winners and I would have less of a strike rate.

Why is it that every young rider has to be ordered/instructed/told to carry a stick on the gallops day after day regardless of which horse they may be riding? Are they all brainwashed into letting their mounts take advantage

Chapter 20

of weak, not in control riders? Animals need firm handling or else you can put yourself and your co-riders in danger.

31 July 2021: Ben Stokes, the English cricketer, is reported to be taking some time out because of mental health issues. Funny how the press and media don't accept that they are a large factor. They build sportsman up then knock them down, then complain when participants are reluctant to communicate with them.

David Dennis moved on this week. We had a great six months and I really hope that he can sort his training career out. But the reality in this game, as previously mentioned, is that no matter how much talent you have unless you have a backer it is a steep climb.

The BHA are currently having a whip consultation to calm the wokes. It will be impossible to keep them happy as their agenda is to outlaw anything that they consider is an abuse of animals which in their small minds is even letting them live. As horse racing goes the present rules suffice and the moment the best horse in the race is prevented from winning because it is in need of a slap to wake it up and make it win then the whole sport finished. A beaten favourite, the jockey asked to comment "It didn't win sir because it needed to be encouraged to go faster and it didn't want to" What is there for the punters to bet on?

10 August 2021: The other day I attended a National Trainers Federation meeting in Pall Mall London at the Institute of Directors, no less. Travelled first class on the train from Gloucester to avoid (meagre) crowds and taxi from Paddington to avoid the Tube. Without a mask all the way there and back. And no one said a word. As usual these meetings open one's eyes to the bottom line of what is really going on. ARC were happy to have the same number of meetings for their multiple tracks but wanted to contribute less executive prize money than the other racecourse groups and increase the number of races per fixture, which indicates more low grade all-weather meetings as the racing surface is cheaper and easier to maintain. ARC was offering 27% compared to the other racecourse groups' 40%. We didn't take long to agree that the NTF position was not to vote in favour of such an insulting offer. The other members of the Horseman's Group were not voting for it either. Funny, that!

As we get prepared for the main part of the new season, it is a time to start working out staff arrangements. As we get older and less able, maybe we should run the operation one member over rather than one under as in the last 27 years.

24 August 2021: A trip to Bangor-on-Dee is fruitless, except for the way above average hospitality. I bump into old Herefordshire acquaintance and I am not joking when I tell you that every time I see him, without fail the first thing he says is, 'We will have a horse with you soon.' He has said that for the last 26 years and I never bring up the topic first.

I'm now searching for a new horse. The Goffs Horses In Training September catalogue has only 165 entered, of which 40 are a bigger than usual consignment from Gigginstown Stud. Every trainer appears to be advertising for staff and there seems to loads of low grade horses still in training. Are Gigginstown pulling the plug on their racing interests because of the so far understated woes of Irish racing and an impending 'hit the fan' big time moment?

1 September 2021: To Uttoxeter with Kalinda today in a vain search for fast ground. I have clearly missed a trick here because all the young jockeys and young clerks of the courses describe ground as a bit quick, when in truth compared to ten years ago they have no clue what quick ground is.

A chance of a new owner! I have known the couple for several years and am aware that they have had no luck and not a sniff of a winner. I have never lobbied them to be owners of mine and was surprised at an approach from them.

8 September 2021: At Doncaster for the Goffs September Sale. I successfully had the winning bid at £26,000 for a new horse for Tony Scrivin. His Weatherbys bank account was flush with prize money thanks to The Bay Birch and Another Flutter, and as this latest horse may be his last, we bought Not Available. Some simple calculations worked out that this was the most expensive purchase in which I had been involved. In 27 years, I calculated that I have trained 195 winners and accumulated £1.6m in prize money, while spending not more than £600,000 in total on horses. I may have been sent some that cost more, but the bottom line is that that is a good statistic. Some owners have been known to spend that on one horse.

19 September 2021: We had a parade of horses during National Racehorse Week with a nice number of attendees. It always a good time of year with some optimistic expectations but also some pessimistic ones about certain horses old and new. It never fails to surprise me how wrong I can get it.

There are lies, damn lies and statistics. How anyone in UK racing administration can see that we need the same number of fixtures as in previous pre-Covid pandemic years is a mystery to me. Small fields with

Chapter 20

less each way chances. More races at crazy times. The bookmakers and the racecourses and the whole business model of UK horse racing needs a serious check up from the neck up! It is obvious. As I've said before and will say again the moment it changed from a sport to an industry it was on a one way ticket to oblivion. I love the horses .I love the competition. I love the sport. I love the business. I LOVE HORSE RACING. I hate the industry. Is that too strong an opinion?

Every day is a school day. A new horse to the yard arrived sporting an ugly wart on his head above his left eye. Jodie had a suggestion to mix flour, salt and water into a doughy paste and apply to the wart. I was very sceptical about the process working, having seen some of the topical dressings to remove warts proving to be very toxic and unpleasant. Very surprised and pleased when the simple, non-stressful process worked perfectly.

9 October 2021: A very proud dad was at Chepstow to witness Stan ride his 100th winner, which was also his biggest prize, on Tea Clipper for Tom Lacey in the Listed novice chase. Job done, Dad!

16 October 2021: For the second Saturday running Stan won a big jumps race for Tom. This was the Welsh Champion Hurdle at Ffos Las. The two prizes totalled around £45,000 and jockey's percentage would be around £4,000. The winning jockey of the two big flat races on the same Saturdays would be expecting 9% of £500,000. Another example of industry before sport methinks!

20 October 2021: Our new horse Not Available ran a blinder at Worcester to finish second. All the pundits questioned my thinking of dropping the gelding in trip when his best form was over further. In the short time we had to assess him he proved to be very slow work horse, so I made the call to drop him to two miles. Fearful of being made to look a prat, my judgement was justified with a very fine run to prove my slow two miler theory yet again.

Racecourse chatter regarding local National Hunt trainers investing in new training facilities and yards made me consider their sanity. Fifteen years ago the winning percentage of prize money that came their way would have gone a lot further paying off investment spending. So far this season Fergal O'Brien has run 101 different horse to win 57 races. His total prize money is £430,000, of which his personal cut would be around £30,000, which wouldn't go very far settling bills on a business of that scale. If you won a big Saturday prize on the flat you could probably get your head back above water! If you are relying on family money and connections to back your training business venture in these difficult times it helps, but if you are beholden to businessmen with rigid contractual agreements to make it work, you are up against it, big time. It is a sad day when a trainer has that much success and personal monetary reward is so poor; the figures clearly don't add up.

21 November 2021: Recent developments with ARC trying to make it a daily feature to stage nine or ten race cards when recent statistics reveal that field sizes are at their lowest for quite some time proves to me that the BHA are not fit for purpose. I appreciate that it is impossible to keep all the people happy all the time but it has failed to understand how much the horsemen have sacrificed and been shafted in the name of industry not sport. It is not all about the levy. Well, yes it could be if the racecourses were transparent about media rights and the bookmakers weren't so obvious about their greed.

26 November 2021: If I had waited until Not Available showed me some ability on the gallops before I ran him, I would have been waiting a long time. His two previous runs had been pleasing and not without hope but I just felt that the better the race the better he might run, and I was proved right when he won a strong novice handicap at Newbury today, the Friday of the Ladbrokes Winter Festival meeting. The Fulke Walwyn Memorial Trophy has a fair history with some previous notable winners going on to great things. It was shown live on ITV3 and we were the outsider of five at 14/1. Not Available won the race fair and square beating a horse that cost £340,000 back in third and the second horse had a reputed high private price tag. I had had previous winners on terrestrial TV but this was my first time being interviewed on course. The presenters loved it because they didn't have the same old faces with the same old answers; just an ecstatic small training outfit smiling and genuinely thrilled to bits. Twitter likes and retweets were high though of course the phone didn't ring as usual with offers of more horses to train. Over the weekend, the breeder of Not Available called me with congratulations and questions about my two miler theory, admitting that he thought I was running the horse over a short trip to reduce his handicap mark.

22 December 2021: Ludlow; winner 190, Not Available. It was the feature race of the day worth £13,000 to the winner and guess what, not a sniff of a mention in the *Racing Post*, but we have been there before, haven't we!

Boxing Day 2021: Wrong Way Harry wins for us, ridden by Richard Patrick. There have been many times when Mrs Shep has been a huge

Chapter 20

factor in an Eastnor winner but this win was particularly sweet. The horse is quirky and extracting a winning performance involved plenty of TLC including travelling loose in the two-horse box. On entering the winner's enclosure covered in mud he was given an almighty cheer by a small number of racegoers who I can only assume were all called Harry. Also, the *Racing Post* gave me more coverage for winning a minor Boxing Day handicap hurdle than the feature race at Ludlow.

New Year's Eve 2021: At Uttoxeter One Fer Mamma won the three mile handicap chase by seventeen lengths. Covid restrictions in England were out of the window, a typical Black Country crowd were chanting like football supporters. It was a welcome change of luck for the owner and the horse should win again. This particular win would later prove significant.

So that is three winners from four runner in nine days and the other runner was a good third. As usual, nobody phones to send a horse. This week was particularly sweet in that Stan rode the winner of the Welsh Grand National. More publicity for the Sheppard family and congratulations from all over the world, yet as per usual no more business.

4 January 2022: The *Racing Post* has me on top of the Hot Trainers table but the morning is tempered by two horses being examined by the vet both having tendon injuries. One horse will probably never run again and the other is off games for at least six months. On a brighter note Always Able is back and another mare that was not expected is arriving today.

Although a prize money boost was needed and most welcome and it looks to be a huge rise, let's face it, it was a very low bar to rise above.

Meanwhile, my wife is trying to keep the sport of point-to-pointing on the road, and it seems that the BHA, health and safety etc have imposed so many rules and regulations that an amateur volunteer sport cannot fund, man or subsidise its existence any longer regardless of the efforts of a hardcore of passionate enthusiasts.

25 February 2022: One Fer Mamma wins again, this time at Warwick. Milo Herbert, an amateur jockey whose family have horses in our point-to-point yard, gave the horse a fine ride. Post-race interviewer Stuart Machin asked for some personal background. Milo replied as if he was on University Challenge, 'Herbert, Exeter, reading Politics.'

31 March 2022: Pottlerath (195) provided Charlie Deutsch with his first Eastnor winner and some creative accounting techniques can calculate that if you add on five hunter chase winners the grand total of 200 winners has been

achieved. Box ticked. The win also nudged us above £100,000 prize money for the season, which is always a fair achievement at our level of business.

19 April 2022: Pottlerath follows up off a four pound higher mark under a fine ride from Stan. It was a good tonic, as Mrs Shep had been involved in a freak accident at the Chaddesley Corbett point-to-point. A hunt horse had a meltdown and trampled on her. Luckily, she escaped any serious head injury, but she did suffer six broken ribs and a punctured lung. If you are going to have a bump like that, paramedics on race day standby are always helpful. Admitted to Worcester A&E, I managed to blag my way in and supply pyjamas and essentials. On the Saturday night shift in Worcester the security guard was wearing an anti-stab vest. Three nights spent in hospital and a very tough wife is home and recovering well.

4 May 2022: Bank Holiday Monday at Eyton on Severn point-to-point. No Dice ridden by Milo Herbert recorded winner 163 between the flags. The jumps season ended with us (just) in the top hundred trainers at 98th and £105,000 in prize money.

There was some publicity recently concerning a very rare 300/1 winner of a maiden hurdle in Ireland. Maybe if all horses in every race were trying then this would not be such an unusual event!

My Irish contact Liam Clarke punted me a horse whose profile caught my eye. Samos Island had some reasonable bumper runs under a 65 year old jockey, two hurdle runs and three times second in point-to-points. Still a maiden, some experience over fences from twelve lifetime runs and just one more run over hurdles was needed to get a handicap mark. We did a deal and the horse was sent over. The previous trainer gave me the heads up that it was a bit kinky (typical of his sire Scorpion) and advised me of some dos and donts. As the horse was racing fit we made an entry for a Huntingdon maiden hurdle over two miles to a) get a handicap mark b) win some prize money before selling it as a maiden pointer. Stan rode the horse and it looked nailed on to finish in the money when the race fell apart between the last two flights and he won going away. Samos Island was a typical Matt value purchase, winning a good chunk of his purchase price but probably devalued his resale potential. However, maybe just maybe this could be the horse that it seems I am likely to be landed with that will be a lucky purchase and win some serious prize money for ourselves. Fingers crossed very tightly.

10 June 2022: There have been five tragic deaths at the Isle of Man TT motorcycle races. Not sure why, but maybe the two year Covid hiatus has

Chapter 20

led to the mechanics tweaking the engines so well that the bikes are too quick for the course and the conditions. Racehorse speed by comparison is unchanged for the last hundred years and although still a hazardous high speed sport with some inevitable death and injury to horse and rider the safety measures ensure that the toll is within a limit.

21 July 2022: Samos Island update. Misguided optimism as per usual. Three subsequent runs proved that his Huntingdon victory was a fluke. Typical!

3 September 2022: Baliyad wins the conditional jockeys' selling hurdle under Ned Fox at Stratford. A royally-bred gelding by Sea The Stars. I guess the Aga Khan didn't notice! I had acquired the horse privately for £3,500 about a year ago and he had a considerable time off. It had been in training for fourteen weeks carrying me plus saddle. The horse had been hard work and continued to return from exercise blowing like a stuffed pig. I decided to take him to the races to bring his fitness on. To my surprise the horse made all the running, but that only tells half the story. What followed was like something out of A Question of Sport's 'What Happened Next?' After passing the winning post the next hurdle comes up very quickly. Baliyad is a very wooden-headed fucker and steering was always an issue. He was being hampered by another runner whose jockey had dropped his reins and who also had zero control. Both horses jumped the impending hurdle and Ned was unseated. His falling body brought down Baliyad. The horse fell awkwardly and laid down for ten minutes, winded. He got up and the big cheer and clap from the racing public was a heartening moment. He was not offered at auction and came home.

Post-race his girth went up another hole each side and the handicapper only raised him two pounds. So hopefully the horse would be fitter and ahead of the assessor.

13 September 2022: I ran Baliyad again today and having made the running the jockey reported the horse had blown up and was beaten out of sight. This time the girth went up another two holes.

A thought: Industry talks on a plan and strategy to save UK racing have been positive in agreeing a way forward but as with our sport they can't get over the fact that one entity has to win, the first one past-the-post.

11 October 2022: Cheekpieces rejuvenated Pottlerath after a couple of poor runs to make it winner number 198 under Rules today. Hereford had done a fine job to provide safe ground with any chance of any significant rainfall

merely a dream. Many people seem to have short memories, as a dry spell at this time of year was not unusual. Pottlerath was Stan's 150th winner of which it was no mean feat for his Dad to provide 54 of them.

A thought: The *Racing Post* is paid to promote Irish point-to-pointing but the UK version of the sport hardly gets the squeak of a mention.

7 January 2023: Not Available, ridden by Tom Bellamy, wins a two mile chase on ITV at Wincanton. A nice prize of £13,000 to make it winner 199. This horse has now won twice on terrestrial TV. The press thought I'd been on a winless drought but I'd had seven seconds and three thirds from twelve individual runners had won a race this season. Unless you are a big racing name, some of these journalists have not got a clue about a small trainer achieving a notable win.

14 January 2023: Stan won the big staying chase of the day at Warwick on Iwilldoit which, soundness permitting, sets up a tilt at the Grand National. Scanning the day's racing made me scream out loud. The novice handicap hurdle attracted just five runners for a £4,000 prize. I won the same contest in 2001 with a horse (first time tongue strap!) called Harcamone, there were nineteen runners for a £4,000 prize. How anyone at the top of horse-racing governance can't see the main problem here is baffling.

25 February 2023: Not Available won at Chepstow to become the 200th National Hunt winner to be trained by the Sheppards at Eastnor. Fittingly, it was a two mile chase. Nearly 25% of Eastnor-trained winners have been at this discipline. It was a Class 2 and owner Tony Scrivin's 30th winner with us. Celebrations were dampened with Tiptoe Tara suffered a potentially career ending injury after showing much promise. So high and so low on the same day!

12 March 2023: Nicky had a double at the Bangor-on-Dee Point-to-Point, Yippee Ki Yay and No Dice to make it 165 Eastnor-trained pointing winners. The Herbert brothers, Milo and Ivor, rode against each other for the first time. On No Dice Milo rode his 16th winner from about 50 lifetime rides. Ivor is still waiting!

26 March 2023: At the Ledbury Hunt Point-to-Point at Maisemore Park, on the outskirts of Gloucester, young Fred Philipson-Stow rode his first winner on A Jet of our Own for another winner between the flags. Three winners and a second from four runners to win £600 with horses that cost £75,000 in total shows how hard it is to compete at the amateur level with cheaper horsepower.

Chapter 20

10 April 2023: Yippee Ki Yay was an impressive winner at the Dingley Point-to-Point for Milo and Not Available was a big race winner at Chepstow. I often refer to the horse as Not Reliable, but his strike rate and prize money haul cannot be sniffed at.

4 June 2023: Today Chato Santana finally got his act together for young Ivor Herbert to get off the mark with a career first win at Bratton Down. Mrs Shep's point-to-point team has been on fire all through the spring. A Jet of Our Own sluiced up by 52 lengths at the Worcestershire meeting and then won at Eyton. He is just as exciting as Yippee Ki Yay, who made it three from four runs and is going to be even better next season.

10 June 2023: Pottlerath completes a super hat trick of staying chase wins within five weeks at Warwick, Worcester and now Bangor.

31 August 2023: Famoso wins a two mile chase at Stratford. A private purchase for £4,700, the horse had been campaigned in three mile point to points but had a handicap mark that was workable. Dropping in trip helped his confidence and provided the Evron Experience Syndicate with their first winner. The horse has a royal pedigree, being a half-brother to Tornado Flyer and his second dam was the mother of Hurricane Fly. Obviously the horse doesn't know what is expected of him or that he cost £175,000 as a three-year-old, but as they say, Elvis had a brother who couldn't sing!

24 October 2023: Mactavish wins a fast ground hurdle under Stan at Hereford for new owner Barry Hawkins.

21 November 2023: Two winners in two days; Passing Kate at Leicester and Mactavish at Hereford to make 208 under rules. That's on top of No Dice opening our point-to-point season earlier this month by winning under a power-packed ride from Milo Herbert at Dunsmore in Devon. And Famoso won his second two mile chase under Stan at Ludlow.

13 December 2023: Two winners from two runs for Johnny Mac. And three pointing winners including a Larkhill double.

31 December 2023: In the spring I was down in the dumps with my future as a race horse trainer and the future of horse racing, full stop. I had suggested to some of my most loyal long-standing owners that I would be calling it a day very soon. By Christmas I was having a rollercoaster couple of months with seven winners from fourteen runners in five weeks, and the point-to-point yard had had four winners from ten runners.

12 January 2024: Two winners from two runners in three days, the roll continues. Johnny Mac wins again at Leicester and Little Pi sluices in at Wincanton. It takes my seasonal total to thirteen, just two short of my best ever.

15 January 2024: At Hereford Famoso makes it three winners in a row. Hot trainer yet again this season! No fanfare or write up in the *Racing Post*.

When checking facts and figures for this book I was delighted to find that I'd omitted some early winners from my calculations. We'd actually passed the 200-winner milestone when One For Mamma won on New Year's Eve 2021. It's a good job I didn't pursue a career in accountancy.

CHAPTER 21

KILLER CHAIRS AND 'THE SLOW TWO MILER'

The sport is beyond saving in its present form. Too many people have put their own greed first and not the glorious sport of horseracing and the consequences are beginning to show. The level of prize money is linked to the volume of racing, so the more races the sport puts on the more income. An owner's son who worked in a betting shop (he loved horseracing and liked a bet) recently left his job because of the ridiculous shift patterns they were expected to work. That is going to get tougher as from time to time there are moves to increase all-weather cards to nine races per meeting. Stable staff are hard to find due to the increasing workload with little free time.

We need to identify the moment that the gambling became more important than the horse and also when it converted from a sport to an industry, and start again! There was a time when every person on the street knew which horse was favourite for the Derby. There was a big mistake made when the usual multiple meetings on a Bank Holiday Monday were axed because the industry succumbed to bookmaker pressure and races were staged which they felt were beyond their scope of coverage and they were missing out on profit. We need to save the sport first and the industry second. We can't stand by and hope the industry is going to save the sport because they are not. The UK authorities have allowed greed to overshadow everything, not just in racing but in all sports and the grass roots have lost. Witness the Spring 2021 uproar about the breakaway European football Super League.

How many young people could have had an interest in horseracing sparked by a May Bank Holiday outing to the local track with Granddad because it was a yearly fixture in the family diary?

We need to put the fun back in. Too many trainers and jockeys are under so much pressure to make horses compete and perform to a level which is beyond the animal's ability. Calling the sport an industry has in my opinion led to horseracing's terminal decline. The wrong type of owners are being fed bullshit by the bloodstock industry, agents and trainers. All these people feed a dream of success from (not) investing in bloodstock – which on an industry scale and business module is fine – but on a 'living the dream' level of one-horse ownership, where the amount of luck required is off the scale.

But on occasions the dream happens and an owner at the very bottom breeds a superstar or buys a 'cheapie' and lives it to the full.

And that is the problem. All the bookmakers have taken advantage of the fact that a certain small number of people are so fanatical about horse racing that their passion provides them with a betting product for which the bookies don't return anything like enough to the sport: in reality they divert as much as they can elsewhere. Very soon these hard-core jumps owners will only have point-to-point racing to compete in. Racecourses have a very good business module to exploit the fun of the racehorse owners. The big festivals and premier Saturdays can be used to maximise returns via the spectacle and atmosphere of horses racing to be first past the post. All other elite sports have given the participants a realistic financial reason to participate. Racing is the opposite. They are driving the bread and butter away and their greed is not good for the future. I know society is changing but recent government interest is in curbing problem gambling and when Denise Coates, the head of Bet365's tax payment to HMRC is over £500m it creates a dilemma for the Treasury and HMG.

If I was taking a new person racing for the first time, I would have a day at Ludlow. Midweek with a fabulous crowd. No boozed-up non racing types, just a knowledgeable local members' crowd. Lunch in the restaurant, watching the races from the roof of the old stand against a spectacular backdrop of Clee Hill, with a great view of the racecourse in addition to a well-placed big screen. It is a great spot but if you have a runner, it is a very awkward to get to before or get from especially after the race to greet your horse and have a debrief from the jockey as it involves lots of steep steps.

To answer my own question, I guess the sport of horse racing became an industry when the very wealthy Arabs started to get involved in flat racing. 300 years ago three Arabian stallions formed the foundation of all UK bloodstock and I believe that it is this concept that the Arabs wish to return to their homeland. The Arabs have been trying to purchase and breed the best bloodlines and have built the biggest and best racecourse at Meydan in Dubai, where they stage some top class racing for top class horses with mind-blowing prize money.

As the online side of the gambling industry has increased since lockdown and the big bookmakers have fewer betting shops open to create turnover, their operating expenses must be much less so there is no excuse for them not to pay more for the product. There will be a small place in the High Street

Chapter 21

for the betting shop community to gather, but as with all progress there are winners and losers.

The anti-doping budget needs to be massive. The racing authorities need to find funds to make sure the sport is squeaky clean. There must be fear that if you break the rules then your punishment is one strike and you are out. Not to transfer the licence to the spouse for twelve months and carry on as normal. Yes, it means a business will crash, but that is life. If trainers know that breaking the drug rules means a lifetime ban then the sport will clean itself. The general public are getting more and more cagey about what animals are subjected to for gambling purposes, be it legit wind ops of which they have no idea or all manner of veterinary procedures to help a horse run around a field faster than another for gambling purposes. The head of the BHA from 2021-24, Julie Harrington, came from cycling which since her departure has endured a new doping of riders scandal and horse racing involves animals and gambling with unscrupulous participants who will do anything to win. Did I tell you that I don't break any rules!

Interesting thought.

If French drug testing is more sensitive than UK or Ireland for jockeys and horses, ie for cocaine and steroids, the positive tests for Zilpaterol (described as a growth promoter for cattle fattening, not a steroid) in Gain horse feeds in 2020 might explain why when I first worked in Ireland way back in 1988, Irish trainers used to praise what a great product it is for keeping condition on horses in training. Could it be that it has been in the system not detected for a long time? And if it is a growth promoter mainly used in the USA it might explain why so many Americans are so obese!

I think and have always thought that £10,000 is a lot of money.

Perhaps I should have been less mean with other people's money. Maybe an extra bid at an auction beyond my agreed limit, what's another £500 plus commission plus VAT? Maybe I should have spent more of the owner's money on precautionary blood tests and endoscopic tracheal examination looking for problems that don't exist. I have never made multiple scattergun entries. I have always spent owners' money thriftly, not made unrealistic speculative entries and tried to keep them informed at all times.

I am often asked if I still enjoy it? And yes, the training aspect of sourcing and winning races with value for money horses I enjoy very much. The business side and finding new owners is becoming tiresome and the striving to compete off a low budget is very stressful at times (like most of the time).

But I often dream about my fantasy land if a lottery win was forthcoming, which would be hard as I don't play that game. It could be so much better if it was easier for many people to win a life-changing £100,000, as most of the money would filter back into the economy instead of stagnating in a bank account. I would live on Eastnor estate, and every single square yard of turf would be preserved as a grass gallop. Certain areas would be saved for use when frosty, depending on how much winter sun it received, and grass cover would be cultured for maximum length. There would be winter turf, summer turf, long gallops, short gallops. I would have a mini racecourse running up and down the nearby Sitch Valley with top of the range portable fences which could easily be moved on to fresh ground. I would buy horses that caught my eye and hopefully a star would emerge. I could experiment with different races and hunches about best trips without having to explain or justify my plan. If I tried something new that failed, then I could just move on and learn. I would have a workforce that were appreciated and paid accordingly and would have a number of special fun horses to give budding young jockeys a chance to get a ride.

And where I am today? I have always been involved in a sport and never treated it as an industry. Treated it as business, yes, but never as a means to make a fortune, only a living!

Optimism

In horseracing optimism is a vital trait. Especially in National Hunt racing. If like me, you are scratching around at the bottom of the pile trying to unearth a gem from a heap of coal, your optimism levels need to be very high. I suppose being optimistic about a cheap purchase attaining our aspirations is a typical dream, but when you need to be optimistic about an expensive horse aspiring to show any ability at all that sets the optimism bar very high indeed!

You see some expensive young horses pitched into low level novice and maiden hurdles which are clearly having a float round to achieve the lowest handicap mark possible. Even then they can fail to win off of that mark. When they do win, a success box in the *Racing Post* results section hails what an amazing purchase it was by a bloodstock agent. Further investigation can reveals the cost, profile and expenses involved to win a 0-100 handicap hurdle at Hexham when it is trained in Lambourn. Then you realise you fucking well need to be optimistic.

Chapter 21

More optimism is needed with the government intervention over affordability checks to try and identify problem gamblers and restrict the level of their liabilities. Less money gambled will have a major impact, reducing racing's income. Point-to-point racing may be the only sport left standing, where passion to keep it going remains. The same with the country's post-Covid woes, too many businesses, too many lifestyles, too much of society having everything propped up and subsidised by the government. It was always going to end in tears.

What you saw is what you got!

In my world there is a definite lack of bling. I make my clothes last, mainly wear wellies and drive around in non-flashy functional vehicles which I own outright. I work seven days a week and up until recently have worried that people might think ill of me if I have a day off. I have sold my services honestly and to the best of my ability. Brief forays into a flashy website have just proved to be expensive and of zero business benefit. Open days are a similar waste of money and to be honest I still don't understand what one has to do to make it. I just wish that it was easier for more people to make a better living from the game. I have been very frugal and, I like to believe, very sensible in the financial aspect of my life. The bottom line is that staffing, the increasing age of Nicky and I, a diminishing owner base who are either passing away or, more likely, disillusioned with the sport being a business or industry is making Matt Sheppard Racing increasingly hard to wagon. There are no regrets, not an ounce of bitterness, just a sense of relief that I have lived and worked in a fantastic sport that is my hobby and passion. I am one lucky fella!

In all honesty I would not have done anything different. There is no doubt that for every bit of bad luck or for every bad decision, something will emerge that will balance the situation. The main positive is that you learn from the mistakes and try not to repeat them. In horse racing you are always trying to raise your game and improve your horses but you often have to accept that there is no improvement left and accept it. I have always considered it a sport first and foremost and was lucky enough to make a living (not a fortune) at it.

Maybe horsemanship is extinct and every training theory revolves around stopwatches, vets and tech. Maybe I have been too honest. Loads of maybes, but at the end of the day I can sleep at night with the knowledge that my conscience is clear. Yes, I have made loads of mistakes and always hold my hand up to them.

Confessions Of A Slow Two-Miler

When we were young, how we laughed at older riders who never let go of their neck straps. At the time we young bucks had no fear. I find it semi-funny that I am now that nervous (but not yet afraid) rider. The main issue I feel is that as one's bodily weight has shifted, in my case top heavy. Your level of balance has shifted so that with any horse spooking or jinking, a sudden slowdown fires your body forward and loss of balance requires Nigel Neck Strap to the rescue. It is OK when you are on a reliable steed, but as brave young riders are getting harder to find and Nicky and I are having to sit astride some young green horses it gives me more incentive to get out of the game on my own terms and both in one piece, well what's left of our human frames. We almost certainly only have one bad fall left in each of us.

As for my future, it would seem that I am destined for a gentle fade away from the dim glimmer of any limelight I may have sparked. In this game the trainers are forgotten much quicker than horses. No regrets, fabulous memories and a feeling that I have been lucky to compete in a very exclusive sport. I wouldn't have done anything different; I just always tried my best.

I didn't even start out with a few good runs that got me badly handicapped! I was badly handicapped from the off!

I suppose the ultimate slow two miler, is me: Matt Sheppard. Average breeding, average pedigree, average conformation going through life at one steady slow pace. Always trying my best. No frills, no glamour. Connections started me out over long trips before realisation of my limitations. Maybe a 125 rated chaser running up to my mark when conditions are right. I was once a reckless jumper, but now I am considered a safe conveyance. I have given my connections some great days out, including Saturdays. Towards the end of my career my limbs are weary, and connections have ruled out a wind op: I don't make a noise but a tongue strap has been a permanent feature, though it has been known to slip on the odd occasion. I have a lot of miles on the clock and cheekpieces help. I have run on all types of ground but these days avoid extremes of heavy or firm. I have raced enthusiastically in racing, punching above my weight in the Sport of Kings. I am the classic Slow Two Miler.

Like a loyal old servant, I am destined to continue as an old stager finishing third or fourth every time at the local tracks for the enjoyment of my owners and trainer to get a lunch and a day at the races. Scraping a bit of meagre prize money for expenses to pay for the jockey, lead up staff and transport. Retirement? What retirement?

Chapter 21

'There are only two types of chairs that can kill you. The electric chair and the armchair!'

My whole life could be described as going in one direction at a two mile pace, and getting to the end come hell or high water!

***

So it is time for a big decision. Our five-year lease is up in November 2024; do we commit for another five years? The spring proves to be an amazing spell with many winners both point to pointing and under Rules. Nicky's yard supplies Grace A Vous Enki to be leading horse in the country. Ihandaya wins four from four and is rated one of the best young horses in the UK with a genuine chance in the 2025 Foxhunters at Cheltenham. A Jet of our Own won the two mile chase at the Cheltenham Hunter Chase evening (a race that I have always wanted to win) and could be an Aintree type. Yippee Ki Yay wins at Exeter and Kelso. So four top class hunters to go to war with. As well as that, owners in the point-to-point yard are restocking even in these uncertain political times. On top of Nicky's fourteen point winners and three hunter chase successes the National Hunt yard equalled its best total at fifteen for the season.

We enter into discussion with the agent to confirm what rent increase we can expect and it proves to be a very sensible workable percentage and all our expected staff intend to return in the autumn. The future of the sport is in such doom and gloom for so many reasons and we are lucky to have enjoyed the ride. With not much deliberation and buoyed by a bequeath from my mother we decide to sign up and carry on. We love horses and we love horse racing.

APPENDIX 1

EASTNOR TRAINED NATIONAL HUNT WINNERS
The right hand column counts the two-mile chases Matt has won.

1	08/02/1995	**Master Eryl**			
		Mr J Pritchard	Ludlow	£2k	1
2	25/11/1995	**Seek The Faith**			
		B Powell Snr	Chepstow	£3k	2
3	23/03/1996	**Oatis Rose**			
		P Carberry	Newbury	£11k	
4	11/02/1997	**Apache Park**			
		D Gallagher	Leicester	£3k	
5	14/02/1997	**Oatis Rose**			
		A Maguire	Sandown	£4k	
6	16/04/1997	**Seek The Faith**			
		R Dunwoody	Cheltenham	£5k	3
7	13/05/1997	**Honeybed Wood**			
		R Johnson	Chepstow	£2k	
8	18/06/1997	**Honeybed Wood**			
		AP McCoy	Worcester	£2k	
9	28/06/1997	**Honeybed Wood**			
		L Aspell	Worcester	£2K	
10	09/05/1997	**Honeybed Wood**			
		AP McCoy	Worcester	£2k	
11	18/12/1997	**Margi Boo**			
		R Johnson	Towcester	£2k	
12	13/02/1998	**Seek The Faith**			
		R Johnson	Newbury	£5k	4
13	13/02/1998	**Now We Know**			
		T.J Murphy	Bangor	£4k	
14	24/03/1998	**Precarium**			
		Mr J Pritchard	Chepstow	£2k	
15	04/04/1998	**Now We Know**			
		S Kelly	Hereford	£2k	
16	13/04/1998	**Now We Know**			
		O Burrows	Hereford	£2k	
17	01/05/1998	**Honeybed Wood**			
		R Dunwoody	Bangor	£2k	
18	31/08/1998	**Lets Twist Again**			
		T.J Murphy	Newton A.	£4k	

Confessions Of A Slow Two-Miler

19	12/03/1999	**Welburn Boy**			
		S Wynne	Hereford	£2k	
20	03/05/1999	**Lime Street Blues**			
		S Stronge	Ludlow	£2k	
21	21/10/1999	**Oakmont**			
		W Marston	Ludlow	£2k	
22	14/02/2000	**Now We Know**			
		Mr J Pritchard	Hereford	£2k	
23	25/02/2000	**Welburn Boy**			
		L Aspell	Ludlow	£4k	
24	07/12/2000	**Deliceo**			
		J Culloty	Ludlow	£5k	
25	13/01/2001	**Harcamone**			
		D Dennis	Warwick	£4k	
26	09/02/2001	**Harcamone**			
		D Dennis	Bangor	£4k	
27	09/11/2001	**Deliceo**			
		J Culloty	Towcester	£4k	
28	29/11/2001	**Asparagus**			
		S Wynne	Uttoxeter	£3k	
29	15/03/2002	**Asparagus**			
		J Culloty	Chepstow	£3k	5
30	23/03/2002	**Asparagus**			
		A Dobbin	Uttoxeter	£3k	6
31	03/10/2002	**Burning Truth**			
		R Biddlecombe	Hereford	£3k	
32	24/10/2002	**Burning Truth**			
		R Biddlecombe	Ludlow	£7k	
33	07/11/2002	**Deliceo**			
		J Culloty	Hereford	£4k	
34	25/02/2003	**Deliceo**			
		J Culloty	Leicester	£3k	
35	12/03/2003	**Burning Truth**			
		R Biddlecombe	Stratford	£6k	
36	15/03/2003	**Asparagus**			
		J Culloty	Uttoxeter	£9k	
37	09/10/2003	**Burning Truth**			
		T Murphy	Ludlow	£3k	
38	02/12/2003	**Deliceo**			
		J Culloty	Hereford	£3k	
39	19/01/2004	**Rudetski**			
		D Dennis	Doncaster	£4k	7
40	22/01/2004	**Deliceo**			
		J Culloty	Ludlow	£7k	

Appendix 1

41	27/03/2004	**Asparagus**		
		D Dennis	Bangor	£11k
42	05/06/2004	**San Marco**		
		D Dennis	Worcester	£3k
43	14/07/2004	**Smile Pleeze**		
		D Dennis	Worcester	£4k
44	18/07/2004	**San Marco**		
		D Dennis	Stratford	£7k
45	30/07/2004	**San Marco**		
		D Dennis	Bangor	£5k
46	06/08/2004	**Smile Pleeze**		
		S Durack	Worcester	£7k
47	24/08/2004	**Smile Pleeze**		
		S Durack	Worcester	£5k
48	13/10/2004	**Allez Toujours**		
		P Flynn	Uttoxeter	£4k
49	31/10/2004	**Deliceo**		
		J Culloty	Huntingdon	£8k
50	12/11/2004	**Smile Pleeze**		
		Mr L Stephens	Cheltenham	£13k
51	22/12/2004	**Deliceo**		
		T Murphy	Ludlow	£7k
52	14/05/2005	**Forzacurity**		
		L Stephens	Bangor	£6k
53	22/05/2005	**Burning Truth**		
		D Dennis	Hereford	£2k
54	14/06/2005	**Rudetski**		
		D Dennis	Hereford	£4k
55	29/06/2005	**Burning Truth**		
		D Dennis	Worcester	£3k
56	05/10/2005	**Young Tot**		
		P Brennan	Towcester	£4k
57	09/11/2005	**Precious Bane**		
		A Thornton	Lingfield	£4k
58	16/11/2005	**Precious Bane**		
		A Thornton	Hexham	£4k
59	04/12/2005	**Moorlands Again**		
		M Bradburne	Warwick	£5k
60	20/01/2006	**Precious Bane**		
		A Thornton	Chepstow	£4k
61	24/02/2006	**Moorlands Again**		
		M Bradburne	Warwick	£7k
62	18/04/2006	**Young Tot**		
		C Williams	Exeter	£3k

Confessions Of A Slow Two-Miler

63	11/07/2006	**Rabbit**			
		P Brennan	Uttoxeter	£4k	
64	19/07/2006	**Welsh Dane**			
		D Dennis	Worcester	£3k	8
65	22/08/2006	**Cheeky Lad**			
		T O'Brien	Worcester	£3k	9
66	02/09/2006	**Cheeky Lad**			
		T O'Brien	Stratford	£6k	10
67	03/09/2006	**Rabbit**			
		P Brennan	Worcester	£4k	
68	10/09/2006	**Rabbit**			
		D Dennis	Stratford	£5k	
69	22/09/2006	**Cheeky Lad**			
		T O'Brien	Worcester	£7k	11
70	30/10/2006	**Syroco**			
		D Dennis	Warwick	£4k	12
71	16/11/2006	**Brave Villa**			
		P Moloney	Hereford	£4k	13
72	22/11/2006	**Brave Villa**			
		T O'Brien	Chepstow	£4k	14
73	23/11/2006	**La Marette**			
		S Durack	Uttoxeter	£5k	
74	27/01/2007	**Star Angler**			
		M Bradburne	Uttoxeter	£5k	
75	20/02/2007	**Brave Villa**			
		S Jones	Hereford	£5k	
76	11/04/2007	**Super Judge**			
		S Jones	Hereford	£5k	
77	27/04/2007	**Swings n Strings**			
		D Dennis	Chepstow	£2k	
78	19/05/2007	**Swings n Strings**			
		D Dennis	Uttoxeter	£5k	15
79	18/06/2007	**Super Judge**			
		S Thomas	Hereford	£5k	
80	09/10/2007	**Try**			
		W Kavanagh	Uttoxeter	£3k	
81	17/10/2007	**Try**			
		W Kavanagh	Uttoxeter	£3k	
82	17/10/2007	**Brave Villa**			
		P Moloney	Uttoxeter	£6k	16
83	09/12/2007	**Brave Villa**			
		P Moloney	Warwick	£6k	17
84	30/01/2008	**Young Yozza**			
		W Hutchinson	Leicester	£3k	

Appendix 1

85	20/03/2008	**Beesneez**		
		S Durack	Ludlow	£8k
86	23/03/2008	**Top Dawn**		
		D England	Plumpton	£3k
87	01/05/2008	**Top Dawn**		
		D England	Hereford	£5k
88	14/05/2008	**Jomelamin**		
		C Huxley	Exeter	£4k
89	15/05/2008	**Super Judge**		
		D England	Ludlow	£8k
90	25/05/2008	**Strong Weld**		
		Mr L Pater	Uttoxeter	£4k
91	29/05/2008	**Jomelamin**		
		A Coleman	Wetherby	£4k
92	12/06/2008	**Lord Alfred**		
		T O'Brien	Uttoxeter	£4k
93	21/08/2008	**Fair Shake**		
		D England	Stratford	£4k
94	03/09/2008	**Silver Kate**		
		A Coleman	Hereford	£2k
95	30/11/2008	**Roisins Prince**		
		A Coleman	Leicester	£3k
96	03/03/2009	**Thethirdoftheforth**		
		Mr L Pater	Exeter	£2k
97	15/03/2009	**Ikorodu Road**		
		N Fehily	Southwell	£4k
98	05/11/2009	**Roisins Prince**		
		A Coleman	Towcester	£2k
99	14/04/2010	**Munlochy Bay**		
		Mr L Pater	Cheltenham	£5k
100	07/04/2011	**Shoudhavenownbettr**		
		Mr J Ridley	Hereford	£2k
101	20/04/2011	**Big Robert**		
		A Coleman	Hereford	£2k
102	13/07/2011	**Turn Up**		
		Mr J Ridley	Worcester	£3k	18
103	05/09/2011	**Pin D'Estruval**		
		C Poste	Newton A.	£3k	19
104	30/12/2011	**Achimota**		
		C Poste	Haydock	£5k
105	03/03/2012	**Ikorodu Road**		
		C Poste	Doncaster	£29k
106	24/03/2012	**Ikorodu Road**		
		C Poste	Newbury	£30k

Confessions Of A Slow Two-Miler

107	27/03/2012	**Munlochy Bay**			
		C Poste	Hereford	£2k	
108	03/06/2012	**Munclochy Bay**			
		C Poste	Uttoxeter	£3k	
109	01/11/2012	**Daneva**			
		Mr J Ridley	Hereford	£2k	20
110	08/01/2013	**Loughalder**			
		C Poste	Chepstow	£2k	
111	09/03/2013	**Loughalder**			
		M Nolan	Chepstow	£2k	
112	12/04/2013	**Loughader**			
		C Poste	Chepstow	£2k	
113	14/07/2013	**Daneva**			
		C Poste	Stratford	£2k	
114	26/10/2013	**Ikorodu Road**			
		Mr J Ridley	Stratford	£9k	
115	21/02/2014	**Loughalder**			
		C Poste	Warwick	£6k	
116	09/03/2014	**Loughalder**			
		C Poste	Warwick	£8k	
117	22/04/2014	**Another Flutter**			
		C Poste	Ludlow	£5k	21
118	06/09/2014	**Another Flutter**			
		C Poste	Stratford	£4k	22
119	02/10/2014	**Another Flutter**			
		T Scudamore	Bangor	£6k	
120	20/11/2014	**Rock On Rocky**			
		C Poste	Chepstow	£3k	
121	30/11/2014	**Rock On Rocky**			
		C Poste	Leicester	£6k	
122	07/01/2015	**Kerryhead Storm**			
		C Poste	Taunton	£5k	23
123	05/02/2015	**Diamond Tammy**			
		T Whelan	Taunton	£4k	24
124	12/02/2015	**Diamond Tammy**			
		T Whelan	Leicester	£5k	25
125	18/02/2015	**Kerryhead Storm**			
		C Poste	Ludlow	£6k	26
126	06/03/2015	**Kerryhead Storm**			
		C Poste	Leicester	£5k	27
127	19/03/2015	**Diamond Tammy**			
		T Whelan	Ludlow	£8k	28
128	04/04/2015	**Another Flutter**			
		S Sheppard	Newton A.	£12k	29

Appendix 1

129	11/04/2015	Modeligo			
		S Sheppard	Chepstow	£3k	
130	06/05/2015	Loughalder			
		C Poste	Uttoxeter	£4k	
131	30/05/2015	Another Flutter			
		C Poste	Stratford	£12k	30
132	11/06/2015	Modeligo			
		S Sheppard	Uttoxeter	£2k	
133	26/07/2015	Modeligo			
		S Sheppard	Uttoxeter	£3k	
134	30/07/2015	Faustina Pius			
		S Sheppard	Stratford	£3k	
135	20/08/2015	Faustina Pius			
		S Sheppard	Stratford	£4k	
136	22/10/2015	Cool Bob			
		S Sheppard	Ludlow	£4k	
137	26/11/2015	Bus Named Desire			
		S Sheppard	Taunton	£4k	
138	16/12/2015	Hill Fort			
		Miss C Hart	Ludlow	£6k	
139	03/03/2016	Beallandendall			
		S Sheppard	Ludlow	£4k	
140	11/03/2016	Kerryhead Storm			
		S Sheppard	Leicester	£5k	31
141	04/04/2016	Modeligo			
		C Poste	Warwick	£4k	32
142	09/04/2016	Loughalder			
		C Poste	Chepstow	£5k	
143	09/04/2016	Hill Fort			
		S Sheppard	Chepstow	£4k	
144	19/04/2016	Mazovian			
		S Sheppard	Ludlow	£4k	
145	05/05/2016	Loughalder			
		C Poste	Uttoxeter	£4k	
146	11/05/2016	Modeligo			
		S Sheppard	Worcester	£4k	33
147	28/06/2016	Derrychrin			
		S Sheppard	Stratford	£3k	
148	02/11/2016	Phangio			
		S Sheppard	Chepstow	£5k	
149	16/11/2016	Bobble Boru			
		S Sheppard	Chepstow	£4k	
150	08/01/2017	Bobble Boru			
		S Sheppard	Chepstow	£3k	

151	11/02/2017	Rock On Rocky				
		S Sheppard	Uttoxeter	£4k	34	
152	19/02/2017	Rock On Rocky				
		S Sheppard	Ffos Las	£5k	35	
153	25/02/2017	Modeligo				
		S Sheppard	Chepstow	£3k	36	
154	10/03/2017	Rock On Rocky				
		S Sheppard	Sandown	£8k	37	
155	12/03/2017	Act Four				
		S Sheppard	Warwick	£4k		
156	01/04/2017	Modeligo				
		S Sheppard	Stratford	£5k	38	
157	08/04/2017	Act Four				
		Mr E Bailey	Chepstow	£3k		
158	28/04/2017	Phangio				
		S Sheppard	Chepstow	£3k		
159	20/05/2017	Orions Might				
		S Sheppard	Uttoxeter	£3k		
160	21/10/2017	Patricks Park				
		Mr E Bailey	Ffos Las	£6k		
161	26/10/2017	Go On Henry				
		Mr E Bailey	Ludlow	£4k		
162	16/12/2017	TB Broke Her				
		S Sheppard	Hereford	£6k		
163	10/01/2018	TB Broke Her				
		S Sheppard	Ludlow	£7k		
164	08/02/2018	The Bay Birch				
		S Sheppard	Towcester	£5k		
165	24/03/2018	Rock On Rocky				
		S Sheppard	Newbury	£7k	39	
166	29/03/2018	The Bay Birch				
		S Sheppard	Towcester	£6k		
167	08/04/2018	The Bay Birch				
		S Sheppard	Exeter	£10k		
168	09/04/2018	Rock On Rocky				
		S Sheppard	Ludlow	£13k	40	
169	14/04/2018	Modeligo				
		S Sheppard	Chepstow	£5k	41	
170	26/04/2018	Phangio				
		S Twiston-Davies	Warwick	£5k		
171	20/05/2018	Modeligo				
		S Sheppard	Stratford	£6k	42	
172	27/05/2018	The Bay Birch				
		S Sheppard	Uttoxeter	£7k		

Appendix 1

173	22/02/2019	The Bay Birch			
		S Sheppard	Warwick	£10k	
174	23/03/2019	The Bay Birch			
		S Sheppard	Bangor	£7k	
175	20/04/2019	The Bay Birch			
		S Sheppard	Haydock	£31k	
176	12/10/2019	The Bay Birch			
		S Bowen	Chepstow	£20k	
177	26/11/2019	All Good Things			
		S Sheppard	Southwell	£3k	
178	13/01/2020	Kestrel Valley			
		S Sheppard	Lingfield	£3k	
179	10/02/2020	Risk And Roll			
		Mr M Herbert	Leicester	£3k	
180	09/03/2020	Risk And Roll			
		Mr M Herbert	Stratford	£3k	43
181	06/08/2020	Getawaytonewbay			
		S Sheppard	Stratford	£3k	44
182	08/10/2020	Kestrel Valley			
		S Sheppard	Ffos Las	£4k	
183	15/12/2020	Kestrel Valley			
		S Sheppard	Wincanton	£3k	
184	14/01/2021	All Good Things			
		S Sheppard	Bangor	£3k	
185	17/02/2021	Hardy Articos			
		S Twiston-Davies	Hereford	£3k	
186	18/02/2021	The Bay Birch			
		S Sheppard	Leicester	£7k	
187	04/03/2021	Broken Quest			
		S Twiston-Davies	Ludlow	£7k	
188	03/04/2021	Innisfree Lad			
		T Bellamy	Haydock	£18k	
189	13/04/2021	Hahadi			
		D Bass	Southwell	£2k	
190	16/04/2021	Schnabel			
		S Twiston-Davies	Fontwell	£6k	
191	18/04/2021	Getawaytonewbay			
		S Sheppard	Stratford	£3k	
192	23/04/2021	Cyclop			
		B Hughes	Perth	£13k	
193	05/05/2021	Schnabel			
		T Bellamy	Fontwell	£4k	
194	21/05/2021	Always Able			
		S Sheppard	Stratford	£2k	

Confessions Of A Slow Two-Miler

195	05/06/2021	Neetside			
		T Midgley	Worcester	£3k	
196	16/06/2021	Kalinda			
		S Sheppard	Uttoxeter	£2k	
197	26/11/2021	Not Available			
		S Sheppard	Newbury	£10k	45
198	22/12/2021	Not Available			
		S Sheppard	Ludlow	£13k	46
199	26/12/2021	Wrong Way Harry			
		R Patrick	Huntingdon	£4k	
200	31/12/2021	One Fer Mamma			
		S Sheppard	Uttoxeter	£3k	
201	25/02/2022	One Fer Mamma			
		Mr M Herbert	Warwick	£3k	
202	31/03/2022	Pottlerath			
		C Deutsch	Warwick	£3k	
203	19/04/2022	Pottlerath			
		S Sheppard	Worcester	£5k	
204	03/06/2022	Samos Island			
		S Sheppard	Huntingdon	£5k	
205	03/09/2022	Baliyad			
		N Fox	Stratford	£3k	
206	11/10/2023	Pottlerath			
		S Sheppard	Hereford	£5k	
207	07/01/2023	Not Available			
		T Bellamy	Wincanton	£13k	47
208	25/02/2023	Not Available			
		S Sheppard	Chepstow	£13k	48
209	10/04/2023	Not Available			
		S Bowen	Chepstow	£13k	49
210	08/05/2023	Pottlerath			
		S Sheppard	Warwick	£5k	
211	24/05/2023	Pottlerath			
		S Sheppard	Worcester	£5k	
212	10/06/2023	Pottlerath			
		S Sheppard	Bangor	£8k	
213	31/08/2023	Famoso			
		R Patrick	Stratford	£4k	50
214	24/10/2023	Mactavish			
		S Sheppard	Hereford	£3k	
215	09/11/2023	Famoso			
		S Sheppard	Ludlow	£5k	51
216	20/11/2023	Passing Kate			
		S Sheppard	Leicester	£3k	

Appendix 1

217	21/11/2023	**Mactavish**			
		S Sheppard	Hereford	£3k	
218	27/11/2023	**Little Pi**			
		S Sheppard	Ludlow	£4k	
219	29/11/2023	**Johnny Mac**			
		L Edwards	Hereford	£3k	52
220	13/12/2023	**Johnny Mac**			
		S Sheppard	Leicester	£3k	53
221	10/01/2024	**Johnny Mac**			
		L Edwards	Leicester	£5k	54
222	12/01/2024	**Little Pi**			
		S Sheppard	Wincanton	£4k	
223	15/01/2024	**Famoso**			
		S Sheppard	Hereford	£3k	55
224	28/02/2024	**Passing Kate**			
		S Sheppard	Wincanton	£4k	

ACKNOWLEDGEMENTS

Huge thanks to Sarah Hibberd who typed up my first random voice notes for at least one third of the script before I was inspired enough to embrace a keyboard. Thanks also to Neil Clark and Jim Beavis for editing, and all the folk good enough to review and give me encouragement to complete the account.

Finally, thanks for the super help in getting us over the final production fence from Nick Craven and Sharon Newick of Weatherbys.